Life After Loss

Life After Loss

THE LESSONS OF GRIEF

Vamık D. Volkan, M.D.,
and Elizabeth Zintl

COLLIER BOOKS
Macmillan Publishing Company
New York

Maxwell Macmillan Canada
Toronto

Maxwell Macmillan International
New York Oxford Singapore Sydney

Collier Books
Macmillan Publishing Company
866 Third Avenue
New York, NY 10022

Maxwell Macmillan Canada, Inc.
1200 Eglinton Avenue East
Suite 200
Don Mills, Ontario M3C 3N1

Macmillan Publishing Company is part of the Maxwell Communication Group of Companies.

The authors gratefully acknowledge permission to reprint excerpts from: "Daddy," by Sylvia Plath, from *The Collected Poems*, edited by Ted Hughes, copyright © 1981 by The Estate of Sylvia Plath, published by HarperCollins; "When a Father Dies," by Bruce Duffy, which first appeared in *Harper's Magazine*, copyright © 1990 by Bruce Duffy. Excerpt from "Little Gidding" in *Four Quartets*, copyright © 1943 by T. S. Eliot and renewed 1971 by Esme Valerie Eliot, reprinted by permission of Harcourt Brace & Company.

Library of Congress Cataloging-in-Publication Data
Volkan, Vamık D., 1932–
Life after loss : the lessons of grief / Vamık D. Volkan and Elizabeth Zintl.
p. cm.
Includes bibliographical references and index.
ISBN 0-02-038107-7
1. Grief. 2. Loss (Psychology) 3. Bereavement—Psychological aspects. 4. Death—Psychological aspects. I. Zintl, Elizabeth. II. Title.
[BF575.G7V65 1994]
155.9'37—dc20 93-35664 CIP

Macmillan books are available at special discounts for bulk purchases for sales promotions, premiums, fund-raising, or educational use. For details, contact:

Special Sales Director
Macmillan Publishing Company
866 Third Avenue
New York, NY 10022

First Collier Books Edition 1994

10 9 8 7 6 5 4 3 2 1

Printed in the United States of America

Contents

Life After Loss

Introduction

A colleague of mine, John Buckman, tells a story of a London man of modest means who was hospitalized for depression after winning the Irish sweepstakes. This fellow was found to be suffering from complicated grief: Sudden wealth meant the loss of his former life. Despite the incentive of his new riches, he could not let it go.

I use this story because it illustrates one of the great truths about our lives: Human beings do not give up things easily. Even when it means trading a hardscrabble life for one of luxury, we mourn what is left behind.

I learned this lesson early in my psychiatric training, but it was not until I met a teenager named Alice that I began truly to fathom the power of unresolved grief.[1]

Alice was eighteen when she became my patient. In the year preceding our meeting, she had lost thirty pounds and been hospitalized for anorexia. Her condition had a curious pattern. On days the scale dropped below ninety-nine pounds, Alice would forget her preoccupation with thinness and eat. When she broke one hundred, she starved herself. When I asked her about this, she shrugged. She had no idea of any symbolic importance to it—and it would be a long while before I did, either. In therapy, Alice traced her problems back three years, to shortly after her grandfather's death. Her "Papa," who weighed more than two hundred pounds, was a giant to her in many ways. He was the most predictably loving person in her life, as well as a leader in their small rural community. Alice spent her childhood playing on the floor of his general store. They were boon companions, the tall, broad-shouldered man and the little girl with one thick braid down the middle of her back.

When Papa developed cancer, the family withheld the news from Alice to avoid upsetting her. When he was hospitalized, Alice was not allowed to visit him. His death came as a devastating blow. At the funeral, Alice could not believe how shrunken and ravaged his body had become. When she overheard the comment that Papa had dwindled to ninety-nine pounds, she blacked out.

Alice's anorexia cannot be attributed only to her complicated grief for her grandfather. It had various sources, including individuation conflicts and her fear of sexuality and pregnancy, but her obsession with the precise weight of ninety-nine pounds was her link to Papa, a desperate attempt to keep the old man alive.

That experience took place nearly thirty years ago. It led me to study how we mourn and what happens when we cannot mourn; when we cannot do the emotional work necessary to let lost persons go, and they roam through our unconscious.[2]

We tend to think of mourning only in response to such massive losses as death or divorce. But mourning is simply the psychological response to any loss or change, the negotiations we make to adjust our inner world to reality. Grief is the emotion that accompanies mourning and we grieve on a recurring basis as we face the commonplace losses that line our lives—be it the loss of an heirloom earring, a hope, an ideal, a friendship, a homeland, a loved one, or even a former self. Loss, as writer Annie Dillard noted in *Pilgrim at Tinker Creek*, is the price we incur by being alive: "the extraordinary rent you have to pay as long as you stay."

One assumes that most Irish sweepstakes winners have an easier time adjusting to their good fortune than did Buckman's patient, that the process of adapting to good news and moving on proves less difficult. But I would hazard a guess that most such winners recall some brief moments of panic, some unexpected tears, some unexplained ambivalence. These are unlabeled signs of mourning, similar to the ones we experience at such tame and happy events as graduating, marrying, or moving to a new house.

The course of our lives depends on our ability to make these breaks, to adapt to all losses, and to use change as a vehicle for growth. Losses not fully mourned—in other words, changes to which we cannot adapt—shadow our lives, sap our energy and impair our ability to connect. If we are unable to mourn, we stay in the thrall of old issues, dreams, and relationships, out of step with the present because we are still dancing to tunes from the past.

In my clinical practice, I am frequently reminded of the ways unresolved losses color our lives, permeating our ability to negotiate even such routine exchanges as greetings, leavetakings, and appointment-making. One individual with a history of unmourned losses will cling to stability and balk at making changes because he or she finds change inherently upsetting; another will compulsively initiate change as if to deny that any person or thing can matter. One person sensitized to loss needs prolonged goodbyes and will call frequently between appointments for reassurance; another bolts abruptly when it is time to go and becomes anxious at any attempt to infuse a leavetaking with meaning or sentiment. The legacy of unresolved losses may be even more devastating in intimate relationships. Those who are unable to mourn may also be unable to sustain long-term loving bonds: Either they hold on too tightly or they cannot hold on tightly enough. This is one of life's paradoxes: If we are unable to let go when death demands it, we are often unable to hang on when life requires it.

Three things are fundamental to an understanding of mourning. First, each loss launches us on an inescapable course through grief. Second, each loss revives all past losses. Third, each loss, if fully mourned, can be a vehicle for growth and regeneration.

As Alice's therapy progressed, she learned the meaning of her obsession with the weight of ninety-nine pounds. She gradually recovered from her anorexia and began to mourn her grandfather. In between our sessions, she spent time in her parents' attic, poring over photograph albums and scrapbooks that chronicled her relationship with Papa. I thus watched her redo the grief work that had derailed years earlier. Around the same time, I was influenced by a behaviorist well known for his work deconditioning patients of their phobias. The two influences combined and led me to propose that certain people with complicated grief could be deconditioned to their losses and enabled to mourn. I undertook a treatment, called regrief therapy, which had the narrow aim of identifying at what point and for what reason a specific grief became complicated.

My regrief patients taught me volumes about the ways we struggle against loss. They revealed to me the existence of what I came to call "linking objects." These are commonplace items that mourners invest with extraordinary significance and which are the key to unlocking certain complicated griefs.

Four factors impair the ability to mourn. The first concerns the emotional makeup of the survivor: Those who had inadequate support for childhood needs or who have sustained a series of losses may have difficulty grieving. The second factor concerns the specific nature of the lost relationship: A relationship that was overly dependent or laden with unfinished business is harder to let go. The third factor has to do with the circumstances of the loss: When someone dies suddenly or brutally, the death is harder to accept. The final factor is the modern prohibition against the expression of grief. We are a culture of death deniers. Rather than face our own vulnerability—that we can both lose and be lost—we praise stoicism and encourage mourners to have a stiff upper lip. We are all set up, culturally, for complicated and delayed mourning.

Yet there is no denying grief; it is as foolish as trying to ignore a broken bone. Nor are there surefire prescriptions to successful mourning, and it is important to know from the outset that this book does not pretend to offer any. Rather, I would hope that through reading the individual stories, the reader will discover a pattern that helps him or her to understand just what loss means to each of us, what alarms it sets off, what old pain it revives.

Death is the most concrete of losses. In our response to it, we see the residue of all our other incomplete, forced, or hurried separations. This book, then, uses death as a prototype to explain how our emotional makeups, personal histories, and circumstances shape our griefs.

The book is divided into three parts. The first examines

an uncomplicated mourning, the psychological negotiations that we undergo after the tolerable loss of someone with whom we had little unfinished business. It shows the dynamics of successful mourning and the transformations and regenerations that result.

Part 2 explores complicated mourning, beginning with the risk factors that complicate grief. It examines the three principal paths of unresolved grief and illustrates these through psychoanalytic and psychotherapeutic cases. The final chapter looks at grief within families.

Part 3 discusses the resolution of grief through therapy, human resiliency, and creative adaptations. It discusses grief as a source of inspiration for artists, and it examines the links between the creative process and mourning.

Throughout the book, I also tell my own story to illustrate how unresolved losses shape our lives and direct our destinies. My life was altered by the emotional presence of a man who died six years before my birth. He was my uncle Vamık, an engineering student, who disappeared mysteriously while away in Istanbul at school. Some time later, a body found floating in the Sea of Marmara was identified as his by bits of clothing. At my birth, I inherited not just his name but the need to replace him within the family. It was my unspoken task to repair the hole his disappearance left in my mother's and grandmother's lives and to achieve the success they felt would have been his. Of course, most of this went on unconsciously; neither they nor I realized at the time how their sorrow tinted our interactions. As I grew up, his name was rarely mentioned. It was not until I was in my psychoanalytic training that I realized the power his presence had wielded in our household.

Writing this book forced me to revisit his memory and so

to remourn aspects of my life. Thus, it made me take stock once again of my vulnerabilities and defenses in the face of loss and deepened my understanding of human nature. All of this reinforced my conviction that loss can be a vehicle for growth. When we mourn fully, we end up knowing more about ourselves and the human condition. We gain not only greater psychological maturity but, eventually, a heightened capacity for joy. That a painful and debilitating loss could leave us richer is an unappealing concept, but true enough. Loss is a brutal gift.

This book is a collaboration between myself and Elizabeth Zintl, a writer who brought to it the many references from literature as well as her own personal experiences. In the course of our collaboration, we made the decision to include my story along with the case studies and decided to write in the first person, using my voice. During the book's final revision, Elizabeth's brother, Terry, a journalist in Rome, died suddenly at age forty-four. His loss profoundly informed the book's final draft.

Many friends and family helped us along the way, and we are deeply indebted to them. Our editor, Erika Goldman; her assistant, Charles Flowers; and our agent, Charlotte Sheedy, were wonderful sources of guidance and encouragement. My assistant, Lee Ann Fargo, worked tirelessly and patiently to get the manuscript in shape. Amy Furth's background in pastoral care and her wise counsel proved invaluable. We are grateful to the Virginia Center for the Creative Arts, where much of this book was written. Paul Zintl deserves special thanks for his generous emotional support and resources.

—Vamik D. Volkan, M.D.
Charlottesville, Virginia

PART ONE

Uncomplicated Mourning

This is the hour of lead
Remembered if outlived
As freezing persons
recollect
The snow—
First chill, then stupor, then
The letting go.

—Emily Dickinson

CHAPTER I

Crisis Grief

The Hour of Lead

In the fall of 1970 as I prepared one morning to go to work, my sisters phoned from Cyprus to tell me my father had died. I cannot say I was unprepared. The last two times I traveled from my home in Virginia to Cyprus to see him, he barely recognized me. He had been a champion backgammon player. On my last visit, we tried to play a few games. For a moment or two, he regained his former vitality and pleasure in the board, only to recede into confusion again. I knew the end was near and I had returned home disconsolate.

In the months preceding his death, my sisters' letters and phone calls told of his further deterioration. I sadly agreed with their assessment that we were blessed that he had died peacefully in his sleep. Still, as I hung up the telephone, I felt exhausted; my mouth was bone-dry, my eyes were filled with tears. I canceled my appointments. As the dry mouth and tearfulness persisted, I was struck by grief's power to ambush. Here I was, steeled for my father's death, someone who had spent decades studying human response to loss. "In spite of everything," I thought, "I'm giving a classic physical reaction."

Our response to loss is reflexive and to some degree, psychobiological, even in the face of a relatively tame loss such as the death of my father, which was expected, merciful, and age-appropriate. His life had been full. By the time of his death, he and I had few unresolved issues and the last time we said goodbye, I had begun to grieve his passing.

THE IDIOSYNCRACIES OF MOURNING

Our mournings are as individualized as our fingerprints, marked by our past history of losses and by the particulars of the relationship. Even within the same family, griefs are highly personal. My sisters, who had always lived near my father, taken care of him until the end, and were daughters not sons, doubtless had different "hot" issues than I in mourning his death. Yet despite common environment and gender, each of my two sisters' mournings were no doubt separate and unique.

Poets and writers have called loss a "spiritual wound" and it may be helpful to think of one's ability to mourn in terms of physical healing. How quickly we mend physically depends on the depth and character of the cut; the same is true of grief. The course of mourning depends on the preparation for the loss, the character of the lost relationship, the mourner's psychological strength, and the capacity to grieve. An infected cut takes longer to heal than a clean one; a difficult relationship or one in which we were highly dependent takes longer to mourn than an uncomplicated one. Even a scratch can be life-threatening to a hemophiliac, just as a minor loss, a move, a promotion can profoundly trouble someone who has had difficulty separating in the past.

I am a psychoanalyst, so it will come as no surprise that I believe that the ability to handle life's transitions begins with our first interactions with a mother or caretaker. If those early interactions were by and large constant, trusting, and loving, we have reservoirs to draw on in the face of change. Throughout life, our ability to give up is directly related to our readiness to make the next step, the security in the environment, the support of those around us, and our track record with letting go.

Mourning consists of two stages. The first is crisis grief, which begins the moment loss occurs or is threatened (for instance, in a diagnosis of terminal illness). Our bodies and minds balk. To avoid facing the death, we flip in and out of denying, splitting, bargaining, anxiety, and anger. The crisis period ends as we assimilate the terrible reality. Many assume that mourning ends with the acceptance of the death. In fact, the second stage of mourning is just beginning. Only once we have accepted the fact of the death can we begin the subtle and complex negotiations required to convert the relationship into a memory that no longer preoccupies.[1]

WHAT IS "NORMAL" GRIEF?

I have often thought that the expression *normal grief* was a contradiction in terms; there is little normal about grief.

To lose a compelling figure in our lives is agonizing. Our reactions, dreams, or daydreams, laced with anger, denial, and splitting, may seem downright weird. Such responses in the first weeks or months after a death or loss are typical symptoms of grief, just as hallucinations accompanying a high fever are common. Difficult to endure, to be sure, but not in themselves a sign of madness.

When should a specific mourning reaction cause alarm? Reading this book should enlarge understanding of the dynamics of grief and also, I hope, share my continuing amazement at the resiliency of the human spirit in the face of loss. However, the best indicators of when to seek help for grief are the persistence of a symptom over a long period of time and the level of distress.[2]

Anyone who feels isolated in grief or worried about the course of mourning should seek out a compassionate ear. As to the standard length of mourning, I am loath to assign timetables since everyone grieves at a different pace and intensity. However, the course of uncomplicated—which is not to say painless—mourning usually takes from one to two years.

CRISIS GRIEF: FROM DENIAL TO ACCEPTANCE

Loss, even misplacing one's car keys, strikes at our illusion of control and predictability. When we lose drastically, our primitive fears of abandonment and helplessness unconsciously reactivate. From infancy, we experience that to be human is to need others. A baby dies without a caretaker to feed and clothe him or her. At a slightly later age, we perceive that we cannot survive—psychically—without a mother's love. Separation, real or threatened, is dangerous. That is the first truth we learn.

And so in the moments after a loss, we are launched into the panic of crisis grief—the period in which we move from denial to acceptance of a loss. Our reactions are a primitive jumble of the physical and psychological. In 1944, psychiatrist Erich Lindemann published a now-classic paper describing the crisis grief reactions of 101 individuals (some of whom were bereaved in Boston's legendary Cocoanut Grove nightclub fire).[3] Although the group was diverse, the reactions proved remarkably uniform. In the hours after a loss, the subjects experienced shortness of breath, tightness in the throat, a need to sigh, muscular limpness, and loss of appetite. They retreated into shock and numbness; other people seemed far away or shadowy. Life took on a surreal quality. Lindemann noted an urgency in their speech, especially when talking about the deceased. Also, he reported that some mourners manifested "traits of the deceased . . . especially symptoms shown during the last illness, or behavior which may have shown at the time of the tragedy." In those cases, a mourner had been observed doing a sort of unconscious mimicking, for instance walking with his dead father's stride or assuming one of the dead man's gestures. This is known as an identification, which is an unconscious expression of an emotional tie with someone. The concept will be explored in later chapters.

After the shock abates, the physical reactions lose their intensity as we begin to absorb reality. If there is a persistent wish during crisis grief, it is to have the loss reversed. That is the hope expressed when we say, "I keep thinking I'm going to wake up and find this has all been a bad dream."

A news account following the 1988 explosion of Pan Am Flight 103 over Lockerbie, Scotland, gave a vivid depiction of crisis grief at its most naked.[4] The family and friends of Flight 103's passengers had gathered at Kennedy Airport expecting a day of reunion, which ended instead in devastation. A clergyman who was present noted that the mourners "shook their heads, pounded tables, pushed their fists in their eyes. After the first awful wave of disbelief, some wept, others grew softly reflective. One woman seemed to be arguing with fate over her lost child: 'I would give my kidneys, my heart, my life. It just makes sense that I should have gone instead.' "

This account provides heartbreaking contrast to my own muted reaction to my father's death which I had been slowly grieving for months through the process of anticipatory mourning.[5] Yet the scene at Kennedy captures the kaleidoscopic nature of crisis grief and the ways that denying, splitting, bargaining, and anger rise and fall. The unconscious mind has no sense of time and is illogical. Its defenses collapse and then revive. One minute, we think we have faced the death; the next we are dialing the dead man's phone number to ask him round for dinner.

I've outlined the phases of crisis grief individually in order to explain the psychological underpinnings. However, do not assume that they are experienced as neatly—or as starkly—as this categorization implies. When we are prepared for a loss, these phases may be so muted as to seem nonexistent; in other cases, they can appear as a jumble. "In grief nothing 'stays put,' " C. S. Lewis noted.

"One keeps on emerging from a phase, but it always recurs. Round and round."[6]

DENYING

Six months after the Pan Am flight crashed in Scotland, the widow of one of the passengers told a reporter from *The Wall Street Journal* her reaction to the news of the explosion. "At first, you deny it, your mind plays tricks, you think the reports must be wrong," she said. She spent the night phoning Pan Am to check that her businessman husband had been on the downed airliner. At 3:30 A.M., the airline confirmed her husband had been a passenger. She tried one last gambit: "I asked if anyone had ever jumped from a plane at thirty-one thousand feet and survived."[7]

Denial is a shock absorber that helps us slowly assimilate an awful truth. Total denial generally bows quickly to reality. We visit the funeral home or attend the graveside burial and those doses of realism make us face the fact of the death. However, without such reality-testing, denial can persist. In *Casualties*, a collection of interviews with families of U.S. soldiers killed in Vietnam, a young woman who had never seen her brother's corpse explained how her denial expressed itself.

> For a long time, I thought, "Well, it's just a mistake. It's just not Paul." . . . I would look for him, really. Then, every once in a while, you'd hear stories about somebody losing their dog tags or something like that, and they'd end up on another body. I felt that's what probably happened, that we had buried somebody else.[8]

SPLITTING

A variation of denial, splitting allows one part of the mind to acknowledge the loss, while the other denies it. A son driving home from arranging his father's memorial service makes a note to get his father's approval of the selected psalms. Splitting is also at work when a grief-stricken widow "hears" her spouse's car crunch the gravel in the driveway; or "sees" him walking the dog as he once did; or "feels" a beloved's presence in the room. The day after a young friend of mine lost her father she came down to breakfast enormously comforted. She had the sense of him in her room the previous night, reassuring her that he was okay and not unhappy with his fate.

Splitting is such a common phenomenon that in some societies, these "visitations" are built into the culture and accepted as part of the normal mourning process.[9] Survivors expect and take comfort from the "visit" of the dead as a last chance to say goodbye.

BARGAINING

In bargaining, there is a greater level of acknowledgment that the loss has occurred, but resistance lingers to the extent that we make psychic deals trying to reverse fate. We replay the last days, weeks, hours before the separation, trying to redo them.

Janice drove down the highway on the way home from her brother's funeral. In the distance, she saw a green mileage sign which she seized on as an invitation to bargain: "If I can correctly guess the distance to home," she told herself, "the death was all a bad dream. And, if it's a dream, I'll let him know how much he means to me."

Along with bargains, we recite a litany of I-should-haves: "I should have paid more attention to his cold, gotten the book she wanted from the library, stayed up with him that last night, told him I loved him."

In the weeks after my father's death, I found myself reviewing his medical care. I recalled that he had an abscessed tooth several years earlier. I developed the theory that the infection had never been properly treated and had spread to his brain, causing his mental deterioration. I was plagued by guilt. Why hadn't I insisted on antibiotics, or had him flown to a U.S. medical center where I could have overseen his care? I obsessively plotted how I could have handled the situation differently. This tapped into a more general guilt I often feel in relation to my family; that I have lived in comfort in the U.S. during a time of political turbulence on the island of Cyprus. After a few such go-rounds, I was able to let go of these thoughts and reassure myself that I had made proper decisions at the time. I separated my irrational guilt about my father's tooth leading to his death from my legitimate regret about the effect Cyprus's political instability had on his life.

These temporary moments of guilt and recriminations commonly mark crisis-stage grief. Certain cultures have even incorporated expressions of guilt and ritualized punishment into their grief practices. In some primitive societies, such as that of the Maoris in New Zealand, families of the dead person cut their breasts to express their loss. If the death occurred by accident, relatives of the dead person were ritually beaten by delegations from other tribes. The visitors also expected to collect goods from the family, to compensate for the loss of a valued friend.[10] Notice the wisdom in these "primitive" people's ritual; it allows transient feelings of guilt to be expunged.

ANXIETY

Since losing someone or something important stirs feelings of rejection and powerlessness, we feel anxious as the reality of the loss seeps in. Anxiety is an emotional fever signaling that our psychic equilibrium is out of whack, just as a rise in body temperature indicates problems in physical functioning. Anxiety is so distressing that we go to great lengths to try to allay the cause of our panic. In her moving book *Widow*, Lynn Caine described how grief eroded her previous self-possession. "I was a lost child and yearned for someone to take care of me, to love me. Anyone." She wrote a rich politician she had once met at a cocktail party, "You are fat and rich; I am poor and thin . . . my husband died leaving me with no life insurance and two small children to support on a publishing salary. Would you please send me $500,000." She received a stiff reply saying that he could not help.[11]

After the AIDS death of his lover, one man described the sensation of "walking around the streets strangely afraid of everything. I've lived in Manhattan for ten years and I've always been aware of the possibilities of getting hurt, but this was different. . . . It was like being constantly afraid of something, but I couldn't name it."[12]

In the months after her sister's sudden death, a friend of mine began seeing danger everywhere. She could not let her teenaged son go on an overnight camping trip. She canceled plans to travel with her husband. The world had revealed itself to be a dangerous place and she was responding in kind.

ANGER

Being left behind infuriates us even if the abandonment was unintentional. "I felt that I had finally let myself trust a man," one woman said to me after her husband's death in a motorcycle accident. "And the SOB deserts me anyway."

In cases of divorce or desertion, there are many different ways to vent anger, from changing the house locks to major litigation. But in the case of death, our social standards do not permit raging. I often think that there was wisdom in the now abandoned custom of wealthy Turkish Cypriot families who hired angry "mourners" to scream at a coffin as it was carried from the house: "Where are you going?" and "How dare you leave us?"

We rarely acknowledge how mad we are at someone who died or left us. Instead, we displace the anger and berate the medical team, complain about the funeral director's diction, explode at the divorce lawyer. In his autobiography, *Timebends,* Arthur Miller described his mother's reaction to the death of her handsome twenty-seven-year-old brother Hymie.

> He walked into the drugstore around the corner on Lenox and 111th to order an Alka Seltzer, and when the pharmacist turned around to serve it, he found him lying dead on the floor. . . .
>
> Twenty-four hours after the news, she still could not take a full breath without breaking into sobs. . . . "That goddamned

druggist," she said, fixing the veil over her face as she looked in the mirror of her dressing table, "if he'd served him quicker he'd have saved his life."[13]

A certain anger is a healthy indication that we are beginning to accept the facts. One wave of anger, one cycle of denial, splitting, and bargaining rarely suffices. These episodes are like a series of inoculations given to build the necessary level of antibodies. "The same leg is cut off time after time," wrote C. S. Lewis. "The first plunge of the knife in the flesh is felt again and again."[14] As crisis grief ends, denial and splitting gradually abate. Slowly, these moments take on a different character. The impulse to "call Mother" becomes the more painful and poignant "I wish I could call Mother." The full measure of the loss begins to be felt.

DREAMS IN CRISIS GRIEF

Dreams tap into our unconscious, help us to fulfill our wishes, work on problems, and express thoughts that we deem unacceptable during waking life.[15] So in crisis grief, the storylines of our dreams mirror the waking life's conflict with accepting the death.

Some dreams of this period are pure denial and, in these, we create happy endings. A son dreams that he rescued his mother from a fatal car accident. A few months after his father's death from cancer, Peter dreamed that the dead man got up from his grave and dusted off the caked mud. "I got tired of being dead," he said, "of just lying around."

The son of sculptor Louise Nevelson believed his mother's friends and advisors kept him from her in the last years of her life. After her death, he reported a dream which restored his mother to him both physically and emotionally.[16] In the dream, she asked him to come visit, explaining that she now lived only two miles from him. "She tells me, 'I couldn't take it in New York anymore. I don't like the people I'm surrounded with. So I made a booju.' That's a gypsy trick. 'I'm not really dead. It's all a joke. You didn't actually *see* me cremated, did you?' "

Splitting is evident in dreams where the deceased appears dead and alive: A woman dreamed that her uncle was sitting next to her at his funeral.

As we begin to acknowledge the loss and feel the accompanying anger, that anger shows up in dreams. These angry dreams help a mourner acknowledge the death, just as anger in waking life does. A few months after her husband's death, a woman dreamed that she slapped him.

Our growing acceptance of the death also surfaces in dreams. A man dreamed that he sat by his brother's grave having a conversation with the dead man as the brother lay in the coffin, decomposing. Four months after her brother's death, a woman dreamed that she was having a late-term abortion; a life was being taken from her. Although such dreams are unpleasant, they are an attempt to confirm the death and generally do not recur after the death is accepted.

Then there are dreams that resolve the task of crisis grief: the need to accept the death. A middle-aged woman, already in analysis, had a chronically depressed husband who often threatened suicide.[17] One night she came home to find her husband's body hanging by a rope from the kitchen ceiling. She quickly cut the rope and struggled to bring him back to life with mouth-to-mouth resuscitation until she could no longer tolerate her revulsion at the stomach fluids rising in his mouth. For a little more than a month after the suicide, the woman reported to her analyst that the same dream recurred each night: the realistic reenactment of her return home, her discovery of her husband's dead body and her attempt to revive him. A month and a half after the death, the dream ended differently. In the new version, instead of the prolonged attempt to resuscitate, she grabbed the knife in frustration and stabbed at her husband's dead body. After this, the repeating dream ceased. Crisis grief ended and she moved into what is known as the work of mourning, the period of assessing the relationship and beginning to cool down the loss.

It seems as if I were pulling apart an endless skein of yarn. . . . I am trying to arrive at the heart of what we were. When I think I have reached it, I realize it is only yet another stage. I must go still farther, travel the space of other remembrance and sensation, rid myself of a kind of envelope each time.

—ANNE PHILIPE

CHAPTER II

The Work of Mourning

Assessing the Relationship and Letting Go

"I'm taking off my wedding ring," a young widow said six months after her husband's death. "I pledged till death do us part, and it did. That's it. I have to move on." These words were spoken by a woman who dearly loved her husband. How I wish that her pain could be eased and the relationship put to rest as easily as the ring slid off her left hand. However, far from ending a relationship, death heats it up.

After we accept a death, we want to move on, to have the pain disappear, and to reimmerse ourselves in life. Yet the emotional presence of the lost person is still banging around in our heads, forcing us to negotiate a new and more appropriate relationship. This period of negotiation is known as *the work of mourning*, a term coined by Freud to describe the internal and external adjustments we must make after a loss.[1] There are two main components to a successful work of mourning: conducting a review of the relationship in order to assess what it meant to us and then turning it into a futureless memory.[2]

PSYCHIC DOUBLES

In his landmark paper "Mourning and Melancholia," Freud noted that we never willingly give up our emotional attachments: Just because we have been abandoned doesn't mean we stop relating to the abandoner.[3] We keep the relationship going by responding to his or her emotional presence, what I call the psychic double.

We carry psychic doubles of all the people and things who populate or once populated our world. These doubles in no way resemble carbon copies. We create psychic doubles the way an artist paints a model, filtering reality through our own vision, needs, fantasies, limitations, and experiences.[4] The psychic double may not even particularly represent a person's character as it would be assessed by an impartial observer. But that is not the point. Psychic doubles represent the psychological truth of the relationship as we experienced it.

The ability to keep psychic doubles crystallizes at about the second year of life. Psychoanalysts refer to this critical achievement as object constancy; it allows a child to keep a cast of characters in his or her mind and enables the child to tolerate periods of being alone. As the ability to keep psychic doubles solidifies, a child is able to be alone for progressively longer periods. We all know adults who cannot bear solitude; the best guess is that something went awry at this developmental stage.

The concept of psychic doubles is essential to understanding the work of mourning. As long as we have an ongoing real-world relationship with someone, he or she influences us and we revise and modify the psychic double accordingly. When he or she leaves our world, the real world experience subsides or disappears and yet the psychic double remains hot, all the more prominently so because of the separation. The work of mourning involves taking the heat out of the loss and cooling down the psychic double.

THE REVIEW: TAKING THE MEASURE OF THE RELATIONSHIP

In order to assess what the relationship meant to us and what we have lost, we conduct a slow-motion review of the connection. We break up the hundreds of elements that comprised the relationship and replay them in memories, dreams, and daydreams. Fond reminiscences stir happy feelings. Disappointments, unmet expectations, unresolved tensions, and unappeased injuries make us feel frustrated, angry, or sad all over again. The object of the review is to find a way to view those elements with equanimity, in order to be able to reach an acceptance of the way things were. The more compelling the psychic double, the more intricate the review and the more painful the longing for reunion. The closer the connection, the more history and affection, the greater occasion for ambivalence and rivalry, all of which need to be negotiated before grief can be resolved.

Each person or thing we lose also has a meaning that extends beyond its obvious external use or its assigned social role. These are subsidiary functions and they add to the loss.

For instance, a Turkish friend's family jewelry was stolen while she was on vacation. As the insurance report indicated, she lost jewelry of moderate value, but to her those earrings, necklaces, and bracelets were irreplaceable, a tangible connection to her homeland and family. She fretted for months. In almost every conversation, she found reminders of the loss and would segue into a rehashing of the robbery, lovingly describing the pieces and their histories. This was part of her review; her way of making peace with an upsetting loss.

Figuring out what the subsidiary losses are is sometimes easy: money, property, prestige, social rank, and comfort are some of the most common. For families of divorce, the family breakup is made more difficult by the fact that money may be tight; sometimes an income that supported one household now must stretch to maintain two. Since in our society, individuals are defined by their marital status, those widowed and divorced frequently report that their loss becomes more complicated by the fact that they are alone in a couple-oriented society.

The intangible subsidiary losses can be the most difficult to assess. C. S. Lewis expressed the difficulty of coping with the loss of the many roles his dead wife filled.

> What was H. not to me? She was my daughter and my mother, my pupil and my teacher, my subject and my sovereign; and always, holding all these in solution, my trusty comrade, friend, shipmate, fellow soldier.[5]

"What is it that I mourn?" wondered writer Toby Talbot the summer after her mother's death.

> Her loss of life? The end of her pleasures? The fact that never again will she drink sweet country water, or bask in the sun

> or set eyes upon her grandchildren. . . . Or is it my own loss that I mourn? My insatiability for her physical presence? The knowledge that she's in the next room, in the next house, in the next city. . . . Or perhaps I mourn the loss of my childhood and youth, of my past. . . . I mourn her record of me. Her support, her corroboration, her assurance that when things were bad, they'd get better. Am I clinging to some youthful version of myself? Or is it my loss of innocence that I mourn?[6]

My patient Jake depended on his father to curb his reckless and impulsive nature. When the father died suddenly, Jake not only lost a father, but he lost the psychic aspect of the father as disciplinarian. Nine months later, Jake applied to a military academy in an attempt to keep his father's image alive. It proved a poor substitute. In time, Jake began to understand that he wanted the academy to do the impossible; replace his father's love. As Jake mourned, he regained enough optimism about life and self-reliance to cool his father's image to a memory. He returned to a public university.

THE DEMANDS OF THE WORK OF MOURNING

The ability to do the work of mourning is tied to our developmental history. From the time we are born, we grow by giving up. The baby surrenders its mother's breast to drink from a cup; she or he loses the security of being carried when she or he begins to walk. If these transitions take place in a secure environment, the child flourishes and is more likely to be an adult who has a psychological model for grieving.

Healthy separations build on each other. Think of it as climbing a ladder. When our footing is sure, the ladder is securely grounded and we are eager to take the next step, we are able to climb to new heights. When the ladder shakes or we are forced to climb too fast, the steps are taken fearfully without a sense of mastery.

Without a history of healthy separations, the work of mourning goes much more slowly. Before we can make peace with the current loss, we are forced to come to terms with incompletely mourned losses from the past. Writer Anne Philipe learned that before she could recover from the death of her husband, Gerard, she had to revisit the pain of her parents' divorce, which she had been too young to grieve fully.

> I had to go all the way back into my childhood to find the insurmountable again, this black of night, this sooty suffering, this feeling of suffocation and being sucked down. . . . There was an octopus inside me: it squeezed my heart and then crawled to my throat, giving my saliva a bitter taste.[7]

The work of mourning is exhausting. We are unconsciously preoccupied with the review and under constant siege from the past. Furthermore, as we review elements of the relationship, we must repeatedly confront our essential loneliness and yearning. No wonder we feel enervated.

Sometimes, the grief itself proves oddly consoling because it is at least one tangible connection to the loss. In Shakespeare's *King John*, Constance explains:

> *Grief fills the room up of my absent child:*
> *Lies in his bed, walks up and down with me,*

Puts on his pretty looks, repeats his words,
Remembers me of all his gracious parts,
Stuffs out his vacant garments with his form;
Then have I reason to be fond of grief![8]

Gradually, the demands of the present begin to assert themselves. We want to be free of the loss and move on. Yet part of us is still enmeshed, not quite finished reviewing, not ready to let go. Wishing grief to end, wishing to have fewer reminders of the lost person, may unconsciously feel like treason.

Such emotional stress puts us at risk for a variety of physical complaints and illnesses. In the first year or two after losing someone to death, individuals smoke more, rely on drugs and alcohol more, and report more aches and pains than those who have not been bereaved.[9]

EXTERNAL REENACTMENTS

Evidence of the work of mourning is often projected into our everyday life. For instance, the legal negotiations leading to a divorce can provide a structure that parallels the psychological negotiations required to let someone go. Ideally, the legal process allows divorcing partners to assess the relationship, air grievances, keep something of what was valuable to each of them, and move on to independent lives.[10]

An artist's work often proves to be an extension of his or her unconscious negotiations. An artist in the throes of grief may write, paint, or compose a work that attempts to assess the lost relationship. The most obvious example of this sort of external reenactment is the poetic elegy. Others of us, less artistically inclined, assemble a scrapbook, organize a photo collage. In our deliberation over what to include, we are doing the work of mourning. "This is what he or she was to me, this was her legacy; this is what I've lost."

Our psychological struggles often are projected onto objects that belonged to or remind us of the deceased. Widows and widowers frequently take weeks or months before they clean out a dead spouse's closet or stop the drugstore from delivering a prescription. Closing up the house, stopping the prescription, sending the clothes to a charity ratifies the death. As long as we are actively engaged with the lost person's psychic double, we may not be ready to make such a break.

In *Widow,* Lynn Caine describes the way she used her husband's Black Watch bathrobe in the months after his death from cancer.

> I'd come home from work and get into that old robe every night. There came a time when I would put it on Friday nights and droop around the house in it all weekend. It was months before I realized that I was getting very peculiar about that bathrobe—and threw it away. . . . I felt guilty. I knew it was simply a raggedy old robe, but emotionally it was Martin still embracing me, still comforting me. When I threw it out, I felt I had committed a little murder and would be punished.[11]

It is a measure of Ms. Caine's perceptiveness that throwing out the bathrobe made her feel as if she had murdered. To end mourning, we turn the psychic double into a memory and free ourselves from its power. Unconsciously, this detachment can feel like "killing." In relationships that do not contain excessive anger, guilt, or dependency, we can put the passing guilt and betrayal in perspective and disengage.

Of course, most of these maneuvers go on below the surface of our awareness. Consider the comment of actress Helen Hayes who noted that, for two years after her husband's death,

> I was just as crazy as you can be and still be at large. I didn't have any really normal minutes during those two years. It wasn't just grief, it was total confusion. I was nutty. . . . And that's the truth. How did I come out of it? I don't know, because I didn't know when I was in it that I was in it.[12]

DREAMS DURING THE WORK OF MOURNING

The work of mourning can be traced through the manifest content, or storyline, of our dreams. Such dreams typically have the elements of the grief work being done: anger at being left behind, the desire for reunion, replaying of the dynamics of the relationship. A woman whose brother died in Vietnam described her dreams at the start of grief work. "Someone would be knocking on the window, trying to get in, and it'd be Don. . . . In the dreams, I kept trying to let him in, and I couldn't let him in. There was no way I could get a door or window open to let him in. I had a lot of dreams like that. I even had good dreams, that he was back, that he was home and everything was okay."[13]

Anna Freud described dreams that occur at the point when we are divided between our desire to complete mourning and the guilt that desire creates because it makes us feel disloyal to the dead. In these dreams, she notes, the dead person can appear complaining of loneliness and desertion. Sometimes the dead person is disguised but struggles to get the dreamer to notice him or her.[14]

My patient Elsa's dream reflected her perception that by completing mourning we abandon the dead. One year after her mother's death, Elsa dreamed that she and her mother were in a kitchen watching a storm outside, and flood waters were rising. Elsa knew that she had to get out of the house; otherwise, she would be killed. But her mother would not leave with her, she said she was too tired to try the escape and told Elsa to go alone. Elsa, sobbing, said goodbye to her mother and left.

The end of the work of mourning can be accompanied by symbolic dreams: The water of a frozen lake begins to thaw, a flower blooms, or dark clouds clear. One of psychoanalyst George Pollock's patients reported that he dreamed in gray as he mourned his father. Finally, as his mourning lifted a "sprig of green" appeared. Pollock writes that these associations dealt with "something coming to life again." It was as though the freed energy heralded "the arrival of spring, when things begin to grow again after a long cold grey winter."[15]

AN END TO MOURNING

When does the work of mourning end? The truest answer is that we never let someone or something important to us go. Because the unconscious is timeless, once we have invested emotionally in a person or thing, we keep its psychic double in the recesses of our minds. As William Faulkner noted, "The past is never dead. . . . It's not even past."[16] A loss can always revive and sting again.

So even when we have fully mourned, grief may recur on the anniversaries connected to the death. These anniversaries can be any important shared occasion or season, time of day, week, or year that recalls the relationship or its end. These reactivations of the psychic double are generally routine and, in uncomplicated grief, they become muted as the years pass.

Some people experience anniversary reactions when their children reach the age of an important loss. For instance, a man whose mother died when he was fifteen found his grief recurring when his daughter turned fifteen. At life's milestones, such as marriages, graduations, or promotions, we often reactivate the psychic doubles of those important to us—as if to gain their approval. This remourning is quite natural; we grieve the absence of loved ones because we would have wanted them to share in the extraordinary moment.

Such recurrences are why we speak only of the *practical* end of grief. The practical end of grief comes when we no longer routinely recall, review, and emotionally respond to thoughts of the loss. We can take pleasure in remembering someone without the corresponding sting over his or her absence. Generally, in uncomplicated mourning this occurs when we have survived a year or two of holidays and other anniversaries without undue pain.[17]

As grief resolves, the sense that the world is full of annoying frustrations begins to ease. One friend of mine realized his mourning had reached a practical end when he flicked on his car windshield wipers only to find one of them broken. He merely shrugged. A moment later, he realized how this response differed from his likely reaction in the past months. While in the throes of mourning, every blown fuse, indifferent salesclerk, and routine mishap seemed a personal affront.

In *A Book about My Mother,* writer Toby Talbot explains the gradual release from grief and the corresponding optimism.

> Piece by piece, I re-enter the world. A new phase. A new body, a new voice. Birds console me by flying, trees by growing, dogs by the warm patch they leave behind on the sofa. . . . It's like a slow recovery from a sickness, this recovery of one's self. . . .
>
> She was the one who taught me to love and to receive love. To be unafraid. In her life and in the way she met death. My mother was at peace. She was ready. A free woman. "Let me go," she said. Okay, Mama, I'm letting you go.
>
> The time has come to separate. For me to go back to the world alone.[18]

What I am saying is not simply the old Puritan truism that "suffering teaches." I do not believe that sheer suffering teaches. If suffering alone taught, all the world would be wise, since everyone suffers. To suffering must be added mourning, understanding, patience, love, openness, and the willingness to remain vulnerable. All these and other factors combined, if the circumstances are right, can *teach and* can *lead to rebirth.*

—Anne Morrow Lindbergh

CHAPTER III

Brutal Gifts

Loss as a Vehicle for Growth

In my clinical practice, I have often observed that patients display new energy and animation as they resolve childhood conflicts. The same phenomenon occurs as mourning ends. We feel an urge to invest in new projects and relationships. We have energy now to spare, we are able to connect again with people around us. We are no longer preoccupied with the past.

Along with this energy comes new maturity and empathy. We understand ourselves better, we know more about what is important to us. We understand that life is short and to be savored. We may be less willing to become enmeshed in silly arguments, petty jealousies, or wastes of time. After his lover's death, one man remarked that he had discovered a spiritual dimension to life, albeit not one that was traditionally religious. He characterized it as having lived all his life "on AM and suddenly discovering there's an FM station." All this represents growth. Not that these gains are ever sufficient to make up for what has been lost. As Rabbi Harold Kushner said of the death of his son, "I am a more sensitive person, a more effective pastor, a more sympathetic counselor because of Aaron's life and death than I would ever have been without it. And I would give up all of those gains in a second if I could have my son back."[1]

Beyond a deepening of understanding, we reach the practical end of mourning with the ability to provide for ourselves something that we needed from the lost relationship. We do this through the process of identifications. Let me explain.

IDENTIFICATIONS

After the death of her husband of thirty-three years, novelist Daphne du Maurier found consolation in her widowhood by imitating the rhythms of her husband's life and using his personal belongings.

> I took over some of his things for myself. I wore his shirts, sat at his writing desk, used his pens to acknowledge the hundreds of letters of condolence; and, by the very process of identification with the objects he had touched, felt closer to him. The evenings were the hardest to bear. The ritual of the hot drink, the lumps of sugar for the two dogs, the

saying of prayers. . . . I continued the ritual, because this too lessened pain.[2]

Ms. du Maurier misuses the term identification which by definition is an unconscious process. However, she sensed the power that identifications have to ease grief. She attempted to mimic the unconscious manner through which we console ourselves by taking some of what we admired or needed from the loved one, thus patching the hole left in our lives. But identification is more than imitation, it is an unconscious process through which—oftentimes in spite of oneself—a person assumes aspects, ideals, and functions of another.

Freud spoke of identification as the earliest expression of an emotional tie with another.[3] We identify with our parents when, from infancy, we mimic their behavior and absorb the experiences of the environment in which we were raised. The little boy watches his father shaving, then mimics him at the mirror. The little girl goes to school and crosses her legs like her mother. We have a whole collection of such unconscious identifications with the aspects, ideals, and functions of those around us. While we continue to identify—or disidentify—with others throughout our lives, these earliest identifications prove most important in shaping our personalities, our characters, and our core values. This process contains something of a paradox. By assuming the aspects, ideals, and functions of another, we become less dependent on him or her. To use an analogy, we model or identify with a teacher when we are trying to learn a foreign language, but once we have mastered the tongue we no longer need the teacher. What begins as an expression of a desire for closeness ends in helping us to stand alone.

A few years back, I took a sabbatical and moved from the lush green environment of Virginia to the more urban Ankara, Turkey, where I had gone to medical school. Happy as I was to be in Turkey, I missed the Virginia countryside. I began dreaming every night of taking grass seed and spreading it around the barren landscape of Ankara. Among other meanings, in my dreams, I was attempting an identification, providing for myself what I cherished and yearned for in the lost environment of Charlottesville.

This is how identifications play a role in helping us to complete mourning. By making identifications with selective aspects of the psychic double, we assimilate the aspects of the other that we needed the most. We take in what was good about the relationship and make that a part of our identity. Identifications thus work as a sort of internal keepsake, motivated by our unconscious desire to keep the lost person or thing close. Meanwhile, enriching identifications have the effect of helping us to separate from the psychic double of the lost other because we provide for ourselves what we once were given. In this way, we are able to separate and end up ironically enriched by our experience of loss.

Some of these identifications are so common as to be clichés: A new widow who never handled money discovers that she has an aptitude for finance; the ne'er-do-well son of a lawyer enrolls in law school after his father's death. Other identifications are more subtle: A widower who depended on his wife to be gregarious and outgoing finds himself developing skills to nurture family members and draw out friends. A woman who depended on her husband to reinforce her sense of femininity may emerge from mourning feeling confident and womanly.

Toby Talbot describes the identifications she made with her mother's strengths as she emerged from mourning.

> Slowly I find myself being weaned from her material presence. Yet, filled with her as never before. It is now I who represent us both. I am our mutual past. I am my mother and myself. She gave me love, to love myself, and to love the world. I must remember how to love.[4]

PART TWO

Complicated Mourning

There is no love without loss. And there is no moving beyond loss without some experiencing of mourning. To be unable to mourn is to be unable to enter the great human cycle of death and rebirth.

—Robert Jay Lifton

CHAPTER IV

Risk Factors

Circumstances That Complicate

Why is it that some of us can make the painful and rigorous psychological negotiations required to complete mourning, while others cannot? Why is it that at one stage in our lives the death of a pet or the departure of a child for college leaves us disconsolate and broken when, at an earlier time, we were apparently able to grieve a more devastating loss, such as the death of a parent or a divorce?

There are no easy answers to these questions; many layers of meaning and circumstance create an individual's response to grief. We do know several risk factors can predispose a person to complicated mourning: unfinished business between loser and lost, external circumstances that overload one's capacity to mourn, unresolved past losses, and an emotional makeup that cannot tolerate separations.

Trying to predict when mourning is likely to become complicated involves an intimate knowledge of an individual's personal history. Let me tell you a little of my own story to illustrate how such risk factors can combine.

Since my professional life has been devoted to a study of

loss and mourning, people often assume that loss shadowed my childhood. I sometimes want to reply that loss shadows every childhood, that childhood is full of surrenders.

On the surface, my boyhood had meager portions of loss and sadness. I was born in Nicosia, Cyprus, the son of two teachers and the only boy in a family of three children. My sisters and I did well in school, and fortune seemed to smile on us. Yet, as I would learn much later, there *was* an unresolved loss influencing our family life. One of my mother's brothers, who had left Cyprus to study engineering in Istanbul, disappeared under mysterious circumstances. Fifty-three days after he vanished, authorities identified a body found floating in the Sea of Marmara as my uncle's from the bits of clothing found on the corpse. At my birth six years later, I was given the dead man's name.

As is so often the case in households where an unresolved loss subtly directs the family drama, my family appeared to have adapted to my uncle's death. His name was rarely mentioned, and I grew up thinking of the accident only as an intriguing mystery. It was not until after I was in psychoanalytic training that I came to recognize how this man I never knew tailored my life and shaped my interest in questions of identity and the role of grief.

It was my largely unconscious role to repair my mother and grandmother's grief by replacing my dead uncle. Their wistful longing for him was somehow eased because he *lived* in me. In the years after his death, they avidly polished his reputation. His intelligence became legendary. He was destined, they believed, to bring the family great honor and restore it to its glory days.

I did my best to fulfill his idealized legacy. I can recall studying a photograph of him in his soccer uniform to try to see, I suppose, whether I resembled him. I realize now I had mixed feelings about being his stand-in. Every child wants to be loved for him or herself, not because he calls to mind a loved person and is understudying an old role. As much as I liked being the heir apparent and the distinction implied by the status, I chafed under the need to be perfect. I had migraine headaches through adolescence, which I now attribute to my self-imposed pressure. I can see unconscious attempts to rebel in my behavior: I made a foolish clerical error on a final exam my last year in school which lowered my academic standing—and thus set me apart from Uncle Vamık's allegedly perfect record. I could never shine on the soccer field. Perhaps soccer was just not my sport or perhaps part of me stubbornly refused to become my uncle's clone. On another occasion, however, I seemed to be reenacting his loss and thereby making an identification with him. On the eve of my departure from the island of Cyprus to go to mainland Turkey to medical school, I was out snorkeling with friends. I suddenly could not breathe. I had to be fished out of the water. His tragedy was nearly mine.

I went on to medical school in Turkey and roomed with a fellow Cypriot Turk named Erol, in a tiny one-room flat crammed with two desks, two chairs, two beds, and a galley kitchen. Erol and I grew close in those years; he became the younger brother I never had.

I graduated from medical school and took an internship in a Chicago hospital where there were a number of other foreigners on the house staff. The total immersion in the Western world was jarring, even though I had been used to city life and exposed to Western habits. Culture shock was compounded by the hideous work schedule and nights of being the only intern on call for six hundred patients.

Then there was the problem of respect. It slowly began to dawn on my fellow interns and myself that foreign medical graduates ranked lowest on the totem pole. We had to redouble our efforts to fit in. The hospital management did little to acclimate us. The formal orientation program for foreigners served only to reinforce our sense of being patronized. For instance, one set of orientation materials had detailed instructions on how to use the telephone, an instrument that was familiar to us all. "Pick up the receiver. Smile! Say hello."

Some American ways confounded me, and I often garbled communications, hampered by my faltering English and lack of familiarity with American medical jargon. (I remember struggling one night to find the proper way to order the painkiller Demerol, which I knew by a different name.) My inability to read signals was never more frustrating than the night a woman staffer, who had befriended me, asked me to dinner. I went thinking she was interested in romance, only to learn that she was a nun. During this period, I lost my first patient, a clergyman whose family met his death with a stoicism quite unlike anything I had ever seen before. In my country, death is greeted with a great deal of outward emotion. The experience left me defeated and saddened.

While I was clumsily trying to assimilate, political tensions between Greeks and Turks had exploded on Cyprus. Acts of terrorism claimed people daily. Mail was unpredictable, but I learned that the Turks on the island had been ghettoized. My grandfather's house now sheltered sixteen families.

Whatever reservoirs I had in the face of loss were heavily tapped that year. I had moved from my homeland; I felt isolated, overworked, and unappreciated. I longed for home even as I mourned that home. I felt guilty for abandoning my people and worried for their safety.

One day, I received news that Erol, while on a visit home to Cyprus, had been killed by Greek terrorists. He was gunned down in a drugstore on an errand to pick up a prescription for his ailing mother. I was heartbroken. Erol's death was senseless and horrifyingly violent. It carried with it the implied threat that any other of my friends or relatives could suffer a similar fate, and I was powerless to help.

My isolation compounded my grief. No one in the American hospital where I trained knew Erol or the tense political situation in Cyprus, nor were they likely to understand the complex emotions that his death stirred in me, including the guilt at having abandoned my family and friends and escaped the island's economic hardship and political unrest.[1]

I learned later that I suffered from what is known as survivor guilt,[2] something commonly seen in soldiers who lose friends in combat. This guilt led to a need to deny my emotions, to deny the meaning of Erol's death, and to avoid confronting the fact that all that I loved was at risk. The fact that Cyprus was remote and correspondence with friends and family was sporadic enabled my denial. I put away all the clippings and letters that referred to Erol's death and immersed myself in work. One day, I realized to my surprise that I could not remember Erol's name. Over the next several years, I had moments when I could not even remember my native tongue. There were logical explanations, of course—I rarely used Turkish—but I now believe that my unconscious guilt caused me to repress.

I do remember one bizarre episode from that period that indicates the degree of my unexpressed anger. A friend proudly showed me his gun collection and urged me to join him in target practice. I never have had any use for guns. However, once my friend persuaded me to try a shot, I took aim at the target and shot round after furious round, hitting bull's-eyes. Just below the surface of my consciousness, I suspect I was enraged at my helplessness, at those who murdered Erol, and probably angry at my friend for getting himself shot and leaving me.

It was years before psychoanalysis allowed me to mourn Erol and to face the guilt I felt at being away from my homeland during such a bloody era. In the meantime, I locked away the grief and no one who knew me in that period would have thought me at all impaired. I cared for patients, married, had children. And all the while, I was busy stuffing down the grief, compromising my ability to participate in "the great human cycle of death and rebirth."

Although I began to mourn Erol in psychoanalysis, I finished the job when I returned to Cyprus for the first time after a twelve-year absence. I made a point of visiting Erol's family and the friends we shared, in what I now realized was a much-delayed review of our friendship, his life and death.

I cite the example of Erol's death to show how factors conspire to create a difficult mourning. Erol died at a time I was fragile, isolated, away from home, and working hard to assimilate a number of other losses. My ability to mourn overloaded. Had I been in Cyprus, participating in the funeral rites (which would have dispatched my denial and given me the opportunity to grieve), Erol's death might not have posed long-lasting problems for me. We had a close and relatively unambivalent relationship. The threat of survivor's guilt would have been greatly minimized.

Risk Factors

The following risk factors to mourning are merely guideposts. There is no way to gauge what the human spirit can withstand and what will break it. Since they have shared personal history, we often expect siblings to have similar psychological Achilles heels. But that turns out not to be so. Parents do not treat every child alike. Birth order, emotional makeup, individual experiences and traumas, and the (mostly unconscious) roles in the family determine the individual's ability to withstand loss.

EXTERNAL CIRCUMSTANCES THAT IMPAIR THE ABILITY TO MOURN

We need time and space in which to grieve, which is one reason that most cultures and religions have funeral rites that address and enable the psychological need to mourn. A death becomes harder to deny after the mourner has been involved in planning the funeral, viewing the body, and forced repeatedly to accept condolences. Beyond dispatching denial, these rituals are also useful because problems with grief may surface during their course and can be treated. For instance, someone who cannot decide on a funeral service, a coffin, or a burial spot is likely to have trouble accepting an element of the death. Often today, grief complicates because we live isolated from religious or family systems.

In other cases, we are kept from fully grieving because of the nature of the death. The shock that accompanies a sudden death can freeze the mourning process. In 1969 alone, all twenty-three patients treated at the University of Virginia for complicated grief had lost loved ones suddenly.[3] Such deaths disturb our sense of the world as a secure place, leave us searching for explanations and feeling guilty that we did not somehow prevent the loss. Other studies bear this out. A Harvard study of widows and widowers under the age of forty-five found that those suddenly bereaved (less than two weeks' warning of a possibly fatal condition or three days' notice of imminent death) had a greater degree of anxiety, self-reproach, or depression than other groups of mourners and were more likely to have complicated mourning.[4] Another study found parents who had lost adult children in sudden traumatic ways, such as traffic fatalities, had significantly more problems than parents who lost children to chronic illnesses, such as cancer.[5]

A violent death has added complications. We commonly repress or displace the anger needed to grieve, because expressing rage feels too threatening, too much an echo of the death itself.

The human urge to deny loss was discussed in the first chapter. When we are isolated at the time of the death, or preoccupied by other circumstances, that denial is allowed to take hold. In the heat of battle, for instance, soldiers often do not mourn because they must repress their grief in order to stay focused. When a loved one dies away from us, and if we never see the body or attend a funeral, the isolation allows us to deny. Isolation is not only geographic in nature. When a death carries stigma, such as deaths from suicide, drug overdoses, or in some communities, AIDS (as discussed below), survivors can be shut out of the social network and denied the ability to express their grief.

Finally, in order to mourn effectively, we must be able to tolerate the idea of losing. Someone who is already mourning a loss may find that the ability to grieve is overtaxed.

Risk Factors

MOURNING AN AIDS DEATH

AIDS deaths resemble deaths from any chronic disease in that the diagnosis generally precedes the death by several months or years, which allows time for anticipatory mourning and some preparation for separation. Yet in many other ways, AIDS deaths are unique, and the stigma attached can make the grief particularly bitter and isolating. *Village Voice* theater critic Michael Feingold summed up the way AIDS has changed the landscape of loss.

> AIDS deprives us of our roles in the customary death scene, intervenes in any comfortable transaction we might have evolved with Death. It is epidemic, and so can never be quite individual. It comes unjustly before its time, sparing or striking arbitrarily, and so can never be wholly inevitable. Because of its arbitrary choices, too, one can never quite call it a consequence of one's own actions, never entirely take responsibility for it as the hero of a tragic drama ought to be able to do. It simply is there, scattering fates this way and that, truncating some lives and leaving others mysteriously carefree, prolonging some torments hideously and cutting others off with the gentle snap of a leaf falling in autumn. Its combination of caprice and control, carried out on so large a scale, undercuts almost any response we can evolve. We react to it with a puzzled, inhibited caution, fearing simultaneously for our lives and the appearance we create—a set of nervous supporting players in a show whose volatile star has unexpectedly come onstage drunk with a loaded gun."[6]

Mourning an AIDS death is likely to be complicated for a variety of reasons, but the dominant complicating forces are cultural. "The lack of tolerance and discrimination against

AIDS patients extends to people who have lost loved ones to AIDS. These mourners often lack support systems; they have no one to talk to about their pain. Too often, they become what we call 'hidden grievers,' " said Kathleen Perry, director of the supportive care program at Manhattan's St. Vincent's Hospital. "Our culture devalues the person who died. What could be more isolating?"

An AIDS grief can resemble mourning a suicide in that the victim is blamed for his or her fate. Survivors get the message that their grief is less worthy of solace, so they do not feel free to vent their pain. When Anne Blake's daughter Dolores was diagnosed with AIDS, Ms. Blake found herself reassessing her friendships, as she tried to find someone to confide in and provide support. She turned to a friend of thirty-five years' standing, but the woman retreated. "I had to deal with that separation on top of losing Dolores," Ms. Blake recalled. "That's unique with AIDS. If you lose a lover or child to cancer, friends rally round and buck you up. If you say 'my daughter has AIDS,' people shrink from you. You become the face of the disease."

In 1984, at the request of the Gay Men's Health Crisis, St. Vincent's Hospital began self-help support groups for those bereaved by AIDS. This important work has yielded the following insights into the idiosyncracies of AIDS griefs, and I am grateful to St. Vincent's for sharing it.

Mourning an AIDS patient begins with the HIV-positive diagnosis, Ms. Perry said, because at the moment of a positive result, life seems permanently changed. However, after a period of adjustment, daily life can resume with some normalcy, she said, providing the individual is in good health. The next major blow comes with the conversion to full-blown AIDS. At that point, patients and their families face the brute reality of death. They have little hope of remission or cure, and so have difficulty maintaining denial, the important buffer that allows mourners to gradually absorb reality. "We all know that people who have AIDS aren't living very long, so that comfort is denied us," Ms. Perry said. After the AIDS diagnosis, grief is marked by a series of gradual declines and complications, as patients lose their ability to work and negotiate in the world. The fact that AIDS sufferers are disproportionately young and the medical community has been unable to find a cure adds to the sense that this is a cruel and unnatural fate, and makes the deaths more difficult to mourn.

If the relationship with the AIDS patient was sexual, mourning becomes complicated by the fear of contagion. A participant in a St. Vincent's support group summed up his dilemma: "This is the man I slept with. My loss is compounded by the fear I have of going the same way . . . and that he won't be there to get me through it. . . . This disease is rampant. It's not a clean, neat death like a heart attack. A heart attack isn't contagious."[7] The fear of contracting AIDS is made more terrifying, Ms. Perry noted, because the physical symptoms of grief—the malaise, gastrointestinal upset, sleep disturbance, fatigue—may resemble AIDS-related illnesses.

Mourning may also complicate if the survivor receives no formal recognition for the relationship and little understanding for the dimensions of his or her loss. An engineer in a St. Vincent's group recalled that his coworkers knew nothing of his personal life, and did not understand why he was so preoccupied by "an illness in the family." His need to keep up a front compounded the physical and emotional stress of caring for his sick lover. Another participant in a St. Vincent's group described the way well-meaning persons trivialized his grief: "People say 'Oh, I know what you are going through. My grandfather died,' or 'My dog died.' Well, this wasn't the death of a pet or an old man, this was my spouse." The pain of having no formal recognition for the relationship is made worse if the dead lover's family does not honor the relationship and shuts the surviving partner out of the funeral arrangements, denies him or her the right to joint property, or otherwise displaces anger on the surviving partner.

Loyalties and issues of care that can divide any grief-stricken family are often exacerbated in an AIDS death, particularly if a family links the death to a particular life-style or behavior. "There's so much people don't understand about this disease," said Anne Blake. "They don't understand that people did not make love or take drugs with the idea of dying in mind." To avoid the stigma attached to AIDS, some families obscure the nature of the illness and keep relatives and friends away from the hospital or funeral for fear of revealing the true cause of death. This avoidance isolates the family, cuts them off from traditional sources of support, and may complicate the grief. "Survivors are left with all the normal feelings of bereavement," Ms. Perry noted, "but also with a lot of anger and shame about the web of deceit they have spun, and about the ways in which they have entered the conspiracy of discrimination. That shame can keep their grief from resolving."

Finally, grief over an AIDS death may complicate because the capacity to mourn is overloaded. Since the early 1980s, certain communities have lived in a state of siege, losing friends daily, never having the luxury to mourn one death properly because the death toll of friends and lovers keeps mounting. In *Borrowed Time: An AIDS Memoir*, Paul Monette describes the way AIDS assaulted his world.

> No one knows where to start with AIDS. Now . . . my friends in L.A. can hardly recall what it felt like any longer, the time before the sickness. Yet we all watched the toll mount in New York, then in San Francisco, for years before it ever touched us here. It comes like a slowly dawning horror. At first you are equipped with a hundred different amulets to keep it far away. Then suddenly someone you know goes into the hospital, and suddenly you are at high noon in full battle gear. They have neglected to tell you that you will be issued no weapons of any sort. So you cobble together a weapon out of anything that lies at hand, like a prisoner honing a spoon handle into a stiletto. You fight tough, you fight dirty, but you cannot fight dirtier than it.[8]

It is no accident that Monette uses the imagery of war. It is often suggested that the closest model to the experience of gay men who have survived the AIDS epidemic is the experience of soldiers who suffered multiple losses in wartime. Yet even that model does not quite fit, because those deaths at least could be cloaked in a sense of moral purpose—defending one's country—while AIDS deaths seem totally random and senseless.

The work of mourning involves not only fully grieving the present loss, but working through any incompletely mourned losses in one's past. Those tasks become impossible when losses overlap. A bereavement counselor noted, "For those of us who live in the world of HIV, by the time you close the circle of grief for one person, four others or ten others have died."[9]

AIDS has redefined the sense of the future and life expectancy for an entire generation. In the modern world, death had been a freak occurrence, an academic concept, to young adults. Now men and women in their twenties and thirties are trying to cope with multiple losses. A social worker, himself HIV infected, described to *The New York Times* the way the virus has narrowed his world. He had "known well" one hundred people who died of AIDS, he said, and now estimates that more than half of his close friends were "sick or dead." When he returns to New York for a visit, he "feels like a Jew returning to Berlin after the Holocaust. The world I knew is gone. . . . I mourn for so many people. I'm in my early forties, and it's hard to accept that this is the end of my life and that of my contemporaries. It's overwhelming. It's about thirty years sooner than I'd planned."[10]

We are still far from having thorough studies of the long-term effects of the AIDS epidemic and the resulting psychological implications. One might expect that the gay community would have been incapacitated by the ravages of AIDS. Yet quite the reverse is true. Whatever the individual implications, as a community, gay men have mobilized spiritual, physical, and political resources to meet the challenge. Their heroism, humanity, and courage have been remarkable, and they represent creative responses to suffering.

UNFINISHED BUSINESS BETWEEN LOSER AND LOST

One of the apparent contradictions to grief is that the happier and more mature a relationship is, the easier it is to let it go, when time or development requires us to move on. This is not to suggest that such leave-takings are not painful; they can be wrenching. But when the relationship was complementary rather than dependent or ambivalent, we can grieve it fully. The converse also proves true: The more dependent we were on the lost person, the more we need him or her to prop up our self-esteem, the harder it proves to let him or her go. The most obvious and cruel example is a child's mourning for a parent. Until a child has completed adolescence (as discussed below), a parent's death is by definition full of unfinished business. The child still needs the parent as a model and a source of love and approval. Similarly, the death of a child can be nearly impossible for a parent to mourn. From the moment a child is conceived, a parent's view of the future alters to include that child. The parent expects to care for and love the child and to have the child outlive him or her.

UNMASTERED LOSSES AND THE IMPORTANCE OF ADOLESCENCE

The central task of mourning involves adapting to deprivation or abandonment. When there are unmastered losses in the past—such as the unresolved death of a parent—we will have difficulty mourning a current loss. Beyond concrete and observable losses, one must consider what psychoanalysts refer to as developmental losses. These are chinks in the normal psychological development. If a child has grown up in a secure, and loving environment, she or he is likely to have had support at critical psychological negotiations, such as separation-individuation and Oedipal conflicts. A good mother, someone once noted, is not only to lean on but to make leaning unnecessary.

Psychoanalyst Martha Wolfenstein suggested that a

healthy completion of adolescence is critical to the ability to mourn fully as an adult.[11] Adolescence, she noted, is a rehearsal for mourning. It involves the same dynamics: During adolescence, the individual reviews his childhood relationship to his parents and family, and relaxes his emotional investments in them (and their psychic doubles) in order to transfer allegiance to his peers and enlarge his world.[12] The key phrase here is healthy completion of adolescence. Adolescents cannot separate from parents when the relationship is tenuous or if parents are threatened by a teenager's attempts at independence. For example, an adolescent may have difficulty separating from divorcing parents because the family relationship is already rocky—and the teenager may feel responsible for holding it together. Similarly, a teenager will have difficulty separating from an alcoholic mother or an abusive father from whom she or he never got enough love and support. That inadequate parenting represents unfinished business between them.

Why is it that some individuals suffer losses that contain these risk factors, and yet are able to grieve effectively? The answer lies in the resiliency of human nature and a little bit of serendipity. The right developmental push—the birth of a child, a new and fulfilling love, a wise therapist—is sometimes all that is needed to help us discover the resources to manage conflict and overcome the likely complications of mourning.

The little boat enters the dark fearful gulf and our only cry is to escape—"put me on land again."

—KATHERINE MANSFIELD

CHAPTER V

Stuck in Denial

When Crisis Grief Goes Awry

Fred, a thirty-year-old gas station attendant, was at work one morning when an ambulance sped by. A call soon came notifying him that his young brother had been killed in an accident. As next of kin, it fell to Fred to identify the corpse at the hospital. His brother's legs had been crushed on impact. Fred made the identification, then hurried back to the station. In the days to come, he insisted the episode was a bad dream. He scheduled himself to work instead of attending the funeral, he dismissed townspeople's expressions of sympathy with the explanation that his brother was out of town on a prolonged vacation. Finally, after a month, he was brought in for a psychiatric evaluation.

In therapy sessions, Fred described his relationship with his younger brother as loving. He gave the impression, however, of buried resentment. His younger brother had regularly one-upped him in the family. During a childhood quarrel, Fred shoved his brother through a plate glass door which slashed the younger boy's legs. Fred never forgot the bloody scene or the devastating power of his envy and anger. The scene at the hospital morgue reactivated his long repressed guilt.

Recall that in crisis grief, the survivor employs a variety of defenses—denial, splitting, bargaining—to avoid facing the death. Then, as the fact of the death begins to sink in, he or she experiences passing guilt for things left undone and feels anxious and angry at the abandonment. When mourning arrests in crisis grief, the survivor generally becomes stuck in this cycle. Even so, Fred's total denial was extraordinary, the only such case I've seen in my whole career.[1]

As soon as he made the connection between his brother's mutilated legs after the fatal accident and his brother's slashed legs thirty years earlier, Fred's denial collapsed. I asked Fred to tell me once again the "dream" of identifying his brother's body. This time, with the realization that the death had indeed occurred, he began crying. Eventually he was able to report how guilty the hospital scene had made him feel, since in the past he had sometimes secretly wished to triumph over his brother. Simply verbalizing all of this was enough to help Fred accept his brother's death and begin on a course of mourning with the help of his minister.

Carl's case, which not only reflected denial but splitting, bargaining, and anger, was more complicated.

CARL: A KALEIDOSCOPE OF CRISIS GRIEF

Some years ago when I was head of an inpatient psychiatric unit, the FBI paid a call. They had arrested a man who had been spotted on a hillside holding a gun trained at motorists below. On the rocks around him, he had painted threatening slogans using the president's initials. This was in the 1960s, when the horror of the Kennedy assassination was still fresh, and soon after Charles Whitman had terrorized Austin, Texas, by climbing up a tower and shooting randomly at the people below.

When I met Carl, a young man in his twenties, I was struck by the rage that simmered under his polite replies to my questions. He tried to show a tough indifference to the sad details of his personal history: He had been deserted by his parents in childhood. His father was an ex-con who took no interest in him. His mother left Carl at her parents' farm to be raised. In the special bond Carl forged with his grandfather, the boy tried to assuage the pain of his early childhood. When Carl's grandmother died, his mourning seemed uncomplicated and uneventful. Sometime soon after the grandmother's death, Carl married and built a house for himself and his wife on the farm property.

Because of his childhood losses, Carl relied on his grandfather for a sense of well-being and trust in the world. Any such dependent tie is laden with ambivalence and anger. We resent being so vulnerable to another. As long as his grandfather was alive, Carl could control his rage, but he panicked when the older man died.

At the funeral, Carl told me, he intellectually knew that the casket held his grandfather's body but he was nevertheless certain that he saw the older man moving about the farmhouse. By itself, this is an example of splitting, a routine experience of crisis grief and nothing to cause alarm. But Carl's behavior soon began to reveal that he could not keep the conflicting emotions about the loss under control. He went to the grave each night and sat on it until sunrise. When I asked him why, he answered that it was in order to keep his grandfather "down." This was a reflection of his anger at being so tied to the old man. But the flip side of these feelings was also evident. He kept a shovel in the trunk of his nearby car: "In case the old man should want to rise from the dead," he would be able to dig him up.

The vigil continued for weeks. By the second month, Carl was exhausted from working nine to five and sitting by the grave all night. In the late afternoons, he broke into angry rages at the slightest provocation. Some of this, no doubt, was attributable to his general exhaustion, but after talking with him, I also believe it was displaced anger at being abandoned. In the midst of one of these outbursts, Carl went into the hills and painted the slogans that drew the FBI's attention. In treatment one day, I asked for his grandfather's full name; it turned out that the president's initials were also his grandfather's. This took Carl completely by surprise. He was unaware that he had merged his grandfather's psychic double with that of another father figure, the president.

Carl's case is a dramatic illustration of what happens when crisis grief becomes complicated. When his parents abandoned him as a toddler, Carl had only limited ability to maintain loving psychic doubles of those important to him. He needed the physical presence of his caretaker-grandfather in order to be constantly reassured. This resembles the behavior of a toddler who can tolerate being away from her mother only so long. After a certain period, the child runs back to her mother's knee and, as psychoanalyst Margaret Mahler noted, "refuels" on love and trust.[2] Much as he resented his reliance on his grandfather, Carl could not tolerate being alone. His grandfather's death reactivated Carl's rage at those earlier abandonments.

Generally anger signals that a mourner is beginning to accept the fact of the death. We vent it, directly or indirectly, and move on. However, Carl had an extraordinary amount of rage at all the abandonments in his life. He was stuck, destined to repeat aspects of crisis grief: denial, splitting, bargaining, anger.

While we were working with Carl, his case took a dramatic and tragic turn. He discovered the body of another patient on the unit who hanged himself. Carl cut down the corpse and furiously began resuscitation efforts. When the emergency team pronounced the man dead, Carl erupted. "God, he's really *dead*. There is such a thing as death," Carl sobbed. After an afternoon and night of crying, he fell into a deep sleep. He awoke subdued and, in sessions with the hospital staff, was able to accept his grandfather's death with more equanimity.

This incident occurred at a "fortunate" time. The therapy sessions had weakened Carl's denial. Such intimate connection to a corpse, the experience of trying and failing to bring it to life, banished the remnants of his denial. Later, he was able to go through the work of mourning. In a five-year follow-up, Carl reported he had no bizarre symptoms and that he lived happily with his wife and family.

ABSENCE OF GRIEF

The most common form of unresolved crisis grief is attempted denial, an absence of grief. In such cases, we unconsciously defend ourselves from painful feelings connected to the loss. We may seem to be adjusting well to the death, divorce, or other transition, but it is at the cost of allowing ourselves to feel.

It is important to understand the psychodynamics of an absence of grief reaction, particularly in light of the modern taboo against the expression of strong emotion, especially grief. We celebrate the stoics, the tradition of Clint Eastwood and John Wayne—men whose faces barely flinch in the face of loss, who bury their dead, square their shoulders, and ride off into the sunset. In fact, such heroes are certain to end badly. Failure to mourn is the emotional equivalent of failing to care for a broken bone.

Psychoanalyst Helene Deutsch first described this "absence of grief" reaction in a classic paper published in 1937.[3] Deutsch theorized that the inability to grieve stems from an unresolved childhood loss. She believed that the repressed emotions eventually find expression. Someone recently bereaved appears to be "healthy" and what our society mistakenly assumes to be "responding well" to the loss. He or she does not cry, show anger or pain. Some time (it could be years) later, while reading of an unrelated loss, death, or separation, he or she is swamped by irritation, anger, or sadness.

Deutsch described an adult man who suffered from a "tormenting indifference" to life despite his efforts to bring forth some feeling. Another case concerned a middle-aged woman who was unable to react to her own grief but went through life finding vicarious emotional release in others' sadness.

Those suffering from absence of grief do not deny the fact of the death or painful loss, they just deny the emotions connected to it. However, as the case of Will illustrates, the grief eventually outs.

WILL: THE COAL MINER'S SON

Will was in his late teens when his father died in a mining accident. The news came suddenly. One evening Will, his mother, and his younger sister were waiting for his father to come home for dinner. Instead, a representative of the mining company appeared at the door. The roof of the mine had collapsed; Will's father had been killed instantly by the descending rubble. His mother and younger sister were debilitated. Will took over all the family business. He could later recall no feelings at the time, no significant episodes of crying or other emotions, just the need to become the man of the house.

Some years later, Will had moved to a large city and had a white-collar job. He suddenly began having extraordinary attacks; his knees buckled under, leaving him unable to stand. He saw a series of neurologists and was put through a battery of tests. He was finally referred to the hospital's psychiatry service.

As I took his history, I discovered that the first attack came on the ninth anniversary of his father's death; all of the attacks occurred in the early evening around the time his father had been due home for dinner. I learned one cause that may have triggered his repressed grief. The father's life insurance payments from the mining company had ended nine years after the death. This combined an anniversary of the death with a real world loss that brought the death home. Furthermore, the end of the payments required Will to again become the man of the family; he took over the role of the provider. Brief in-patient therapy was all Will needed to put his grief back on course. His symptoms disappeared.

Because those suffering from absence of grief are surface stoics, it is hard to gauge just how many of us utilize such defenses. In the third volume of his series *Attachment and Loss*, psychoanalyst John Bowlby detailed clues to absence of grief reactions.

> Adults who show prolonged absences of conscious grieving are commonly self-sufficient people, proud of their independence and self-control, scornful of sentiment; tears they regard as a weakness. After a loss, they take pride in carrying on as though nothing had happened, are busy and efficient and may appear to be coping splendidly. But a sensitive observer notes that they are tense and often short-tempered. No references to the loss are volunteered, reminders are avoided. . . . Naturally there are variants to the condition. . . . In some people cheerfulness seems a little forced; others are wooden and too formal.[4]

Bowlby cites the case of Mr. AA drawn from a National Institute of Mental Health study of the parents of fatally ill children.

A thirty-three-year-old salesman, father of a child with leukemia, Mr. AA was cheerful, responsive, and eager to please. He visited the hospital every day. The researchers and staff found him outgoing but noticed he avoided spending time with his son. He said he "found it depressing to see all the other sick children." One weekend, Mr. AA had to spend time alone with the boy. In that weekend's research interview, psychiatrists expected him to show at least some anxiety, signs of grief or distress. To their surprise, Mr. AA was his usual high-spirited self and gave no evidence of active grieving. However, the study investigated the effects of prolonged stress on endocrine secretion rates and Mr. AA's results proved startling. His rate soared to more than double its usual level, suggesting that the experience elicited the physiological components of mourning even though the psychological and behavioral elements were absent.

Although these stoics will not permit any discussion of

their sorrow, Bowlby notes, they often become deeply concerned with the welfare of others, becoming what he terms "a compulsive caregiver," giving to others the tenderness which they deny themselves.

In *The Accidental Tourist*, novelist Anne Tyler provides an affecting depiction of an absence of grief reaction in the character of Macon Leary. Macon's approach to life is to protect himself, a posture that stiffened after his son's death in a freak shooting at a fast-food restaurant. As his wife tells him:

> Everything that might touch or upset you or disrupt you, you've given up without a murmur. . . . And when Ethan died, . . . you emptied his closet and his bureau as if you couldn't be rid of him soon enough. You kept offering people his junk in the basement, stilts and sleds and skateboards, and you couldn't understand why they didn't accept them. . . . There's something so muffled about the way you experience things, I mean love or grief or anything; it's like you're trying to slip through life unchanged.[5]

Tyler helps Macon Leary out with just the sort of lucky developmental push that I discussed at the end of the chapter on risk factors. The love of a warmhearted dog trainer and her son gradually breaks down Macon's resistance and allows him to grieve the loss of his son. He thaws out.

A force so evil ruled heaven and earth that it altered the natural order of the universe, and the heart of my mother was floating in the smoke-filled sky of Auschwitz. I have tried to rub the smoke out of my vision for forty years now, but my eyes are still burning, Mother.

—ISABELLA LEITNER

CHAPTER VI

Perennial Mourners

When Loss Has No Resolution

When Queen Victoria's beloved Albert died, her biographer Lytton Strachey tells us, the monarch let out "a long wild shriek that rang through the terror-stricken castle," then settled into a deep gloom. She ordered that his clothes be laid out nightly and that his chamber pot be scoured every day. She referred to him in the present tense. She clung to his outmoded opinions on foreign affairs, stopped attending ceremonial events, and draped herself in deep mourning for the nearly four decades she outlived him.[1]

Even in an era when people luxuriated in their mourning, Victoria took bereavement to new heights. She had statues erected of Albert throughout the country and organized a fund for a permanent national memorial. The result stands today in Kensington garden, a massive structure two hundred feet in length, containing more than 170 marble figures.

It might just as well stand as a monument to the Queen

of perennial mourning. Perennial mourners are locked in a chronic review of the lost relationship in an attempt to find some resolution to it. The resolution is never reached because the loss is simply too hot to cool down. In some cases, perennial mourning is to be expected. The loss is of such dimensions that the mourner can never make peace with it, such as the life-altering horror of the Holocaust or the brutal and sudden loss of a child.

Years after the event, perennial mourners show signs and symptoms that typically disappear within a year or two in an uncomplicated grief. You've seen movies based on the dynamic, such as *Truly, Madly, Deeply*; *Dona Flor and Her Two Husbands*; and *Field of Dreams*. These center on characters who, due to unfinished aspects of the relationships, retain unusually strong preoccupations with the dead.

Playwright Arthur Miller describes meeting his dead Uncle Hymie's former wife and observing her lingering obsession with a man who had died decades earlier.

> She seemed like some legendary bird whose slain mate remains an image in her eye forever. . . . How terrible it seemed then that she should have been so transfixed by a man for a lifetime, a man she had known for hardly more than a year, yet as she leaned into the mirror pressing her roughed lips together it seemed she was preparing to meet him tonight in her empty apartment.[2]

The degree of fixation varies; in some perennial mourners it is repressed. Many perennial mourners remarry and have successful careers, but part of their energy is elsewhere. Often, a glimpse of their preoccupation surfaces in slips of the tongue. The dead may be referred to in the present tense, such as "Alexander has curly hair"; "George hates broccoli."

A man I know refers to his first wife as his "wife," even though they have been divorced ten years; his present wife is his "second wife." In his bookcase, the wedding album from his first wedding sits alongside the album from the second. Decades after her husband's death, Queen Victoria would open a small brooch with Albert's likeness in it to show "him" an interesting view. Others keep a corner of the house as a sort of shrine to the dead, have a "sense" that their dead are with them, or not far away. They often maintain a lively interest in reincarnation, Ouija boards, and other supernatural subjects.

Perennial mourners keep up rituals that appear to be merely sentimental tributes to the dead, yet a closer look reveals that an anxiety-laden relationship is ongoing. After his elderly father died, one of my patients kept his father's old car and spent large sums maintaining it, even though he never put a key in the ignition.

My patient Bernard revealed, in a fairly dramatic way, his need to keep the relationship with his cantankerous wife ongoing. In the years after her death, Bernard became fixed on the idea that his wife was unhappy in her grave. He moved her body from its original plot to a spot outside his bedroom window. Shortly afterward, he decided she would be more comfortable with a pastoral setting, and moved her to a cemetery in the countryside. When he was planning a third move, his family insisted he enter treatment. His preoccupation mirrored the struggle he had staying faithful to his wife during the years when she was an invalid who became ill-tempered and mean. After her death, he felt guilty for ever feeling resentful and disloyal to her. That guilt (and the repressed anger he felt at being made to feel guilty) kept him from cooling down her psychic double. By worrying about her grave, he kept the dynamics—being burdened and resentful yet guilty for those feelings—of the marriage going.

AMBIVALENCE

The perennial mourner wants to undo the loss and be reunited with the lost other, yet he also wants to have the lost relationship be less preoccupying. This sets up a conflict between the longing to save the lost other and the urge to be rid of him or her. As writer Bruce Duffy explained,

> The truth is, we don't *want* the dead to return, that's our dark secret and the bitter root of our confusion. Oh, Mother, so many years, I've spent running and never catching up, cursing you because I could neither catch you nor kill you as a memory, powerless ever to get free.[3]

DREAMS OF PERENNIAL MOURNERS

Perennial mourners spend their lives having dreams of the sort that usually pass quickly in uncomplicated grief. These mourners' dreams have three common story lines. The first reflects the sense of being immobilized and is composed of one lifeless tableau after another. One of my patients dreamed of a framed painting of a tree. When I asked him to describe it, it turned out to be a weeping willow, an apt metaphor for his contained and fixed grief. Another likened his dreams to watching sliced bread fall out of its wrapper.

The second category of dreams directly reflects the illusion that the loss can be reversed; a corpse lies in its coffin sweating profusely or a long-buried body is found to be intact. These dreams reflect a sense that someone pronounced dead is, in fact, alive. They also reflect the mourner's ambivalence; he or she wants the dead to be dead so that they can finish grieving, but the dead person lives on.

The third sort of dream shows the lost person in jeopardy or fighting for his life. My patient Bill dreamed frequently of trying to pull his father from a burning car. The dream inevitably ended before the rescue was completed. Bill would wake full of anxiety, left once again without a resolution to his loss.

WHEN THE DEAD LIVE ON

Some perennial mourners do more than just dream of the dead; they experience the lost person as a constant inner companion. This is not unlike children who have an imaginary playmate, a condition that may be temporary or an indication of trouble. The perennial mourner relates and responds to the dead person in much the same manner. He *feels* him or her to be present and may even feel that he is actually carrying the spirit within.

This results from the inability to resolve the conflict with the loss. As we have discussed, separation makes the psychic double of the lost relationship heat up and become prominent in the survivor's unconscious. In a routine work of mourning through the review and the process of identifications, the double is cooled down and assimilated. The mourner is thus able to separate from the relationship. Perennial mourners are unable to separate; the psychic double becomes intrusive.

It can be an influential presence in the mourner's life; psychoanalysts call such an emotional presence an introject. An introject is often experienced by the mourner as a disembodied voice; sometimes it is experienced as a miniature of the dead person but it truly represents the dynamics of the lost relationship.

The Pulitzer Prize–winning journalist Russell Baker writes in his memoir of the continuing influence of "my mother racketing around in my head." There is no indication that Russell Baker has a disturbing introject, or that he does anything more than summon up his mother as a sort of demanding muse. Yet he explains the dynamic so effectively that I am borrowing his description to explain how an introject can be an influential presence, in his case a positive one.

> My mother, dead now to the world but still roaming free in my mind, wakes me some mornings before daybreak. "If there's one thing I can't stand, it's a quitter." I have heard her say that all my life. Now, lying in bed, coming awake in the dark, I feel the fury of her energy fighting the good-for-nothing idler within me who wants to go back to sleep instead of tackling the brave new day.[4]

When perennial mourners report introjects, the descriptions are somewhat less inspiring. Consider the case of Ted.

An engaging young businessman, Ted once came to see me for a diagnostic interview. His life was outwardly in good shape, he said, except for problems that he was having with his bossy older brother, Randolph. On the way to work, and increasingly on the way home, Randolph would lecture Ted. Ted found these advice-laden monologues stressful after a long day at the office.

My first impression was that Randolph lived with Ted and

his family. Halfway into the session, however, Ted mentioned that Randolph had been killed several years earlier in a hunting accident. The assumption that Ted lived with Randolph was correct, in a sense, since Ted felt that Randolph's head was lodged in his chest. When mad at Randolph, Ted would visualize a bullet in his brother's forehead in an unconscious attempt to reenact the death and have him stay dead. But Ted could not successfully "kill off" his dead brother. I don't know what happened to Ted because I never saw him again.

My patient Phyllis's grief at one point produced an introject similar to Ted's. As time passed, she externalized the drama. Her case thus illustrates both the concept of introjects and linking objects.

PHYLLIS

Phyllis was in her early twenties when her younger, mentally retarded sister, Cara, died. Cara had been institutionalized since her teenage years; she came home only on weekend passes. On one such visit, Cara slipped on the stairs and broke her neck, dying instantly. Phyllis had been out on a first date the evening of the accident. Sad as she was over Cara, she would later recall guiltily that it irritated her that the death might spoil her new romance. Phyllis found her mind wandering to her new boyfriend during the funeral. Between hymns, she calculated how soon she could be seen out dancing again without appearing callous.

In the weeks after the funeral, Phyllis was flooded with both consoling and difficult memories: how as a child she fantasized she would cure Cara, how Cara's illness had spoiled Phyllis's fun. She felt regret for agreeing with her parents' decision to institutionalize Cara. Gradually, however, Phyllis felt she was adapting to the death. After all, she told herself, Cara had effectively "left" when she was institutionalized.

A few months later, Phyllis was driving in the country with a friend when the car hit a horse that had bolted in front of them. The animal hurtled into the air. The women watched in horror as the horse hit the asphalt and broke its neck. While her friend went to call the police, Phyllis watched the animal thrash about in its death throes. She felt helpless and tormented by the sense that fate was grotesquely restaging her sister's death. She noticed some rocks by the roadside, and reflected that she would have to be as "hard as these rocks" to bear up under such a scene. As the horse gave its last gasp, Phyllis picked up one of the flat stones, kept it in her hand for a while, then dropped it into her pocket. When she got home, she put it in a box in her bedroom closet.

Over the next few years, Phyllis had the sense that Cara was "around." This sense was particularly strong on weekends, the times Cara had returned home. Phyllis would keep an eye out for signs of her sister, yet at the same time was petrified that she might find her. Once Phyllis heard a thud outside her apartment window. She felt sure that it was Cara falling from a nearby tree, even though she intellectually knew that this was impossible.

Over time, Phyllis developed the sensation that somewhere within herself she carried a miniature of Cara lying at the foot of the stairs. At work, Phyllis would have the urge to use her foot to nudge Cara awake, although sometimes these nudges turned into sharp kicks and Phyllis felt guilty. Phyllis could often pinpoint what summoned Cara's presence. For instance, once when she used the sexual term *necking*, she flashed to her sister's broken neck.

Phyllis felt herself to be normal except for the fact of Cara's "presence." She spoke of Cara in the present tense and, during the year before she saw me, had joined a group that tried to contact the dead.

Note that Phyllis fits perfectly the profile of a perennial mourner: She did not particularly feel guilty about her relationship with her sister nor did she exhibit the low self-esteem and self-reproach of a depressed engulfed mourner. Had she been only six months to a year into her grief, I would not have found her symptoms unusual.

However, Phyllis sought my help when she realized how much energy she was expending relating to a dead person. She wanted to get on with her life.

In therapy, I encouraged Phyllis to speak about her childhood with Cara. She described her delight with her sister during the early years, when the retardation was less apparent and less of an intrusion on the family. When Phyllis learned the seriousness of Cara's condition, she spent hours dreaming of curing her sister. When Cara was hospitalized and Phyllis realized no cure was possible, she began to grieve, even though this grief was mixed with guilty relief that Cara was gone. So Phyllis's relationship to her sister was full of ambivalence, which made the death difficult to mourn.

In psychoanalytic psychotherapy, a patient uses the therapist to replay childhood expectations, conflicts, wishes, and defenses through a process called transference. One of the feelings Phyllis attributed to me was that I was constantly busy, too busy to listen to her even during our sessions. As she worked through these feelings, she recognized that Cara's presence had, for many good reasons, overburdened her parents and made them too busy. She began to accept and understand her resentment of Cara, which lessened her guilt. As her understanding unfolded, Phyllis could cool down the hot elements in her relationship with Cara and move through a normal work of mourning.

LINKING OBJECTS: PHYLLIS'S ROCK

One of Phyllis's questions for me concerned the importance of the flat rock that she picked up on the side of the road the day her car hit the horse. She recognized that it held some kind of magic for her and felt compelled to keep it. Although she disliked looking at it, she knew at all times where it was. The hardness of the flat smooth stone reverberated for her on several levels. It recalled Cara to her: the flatness of Cara's chest, as well as a defensive joke their brother used to make about Cara having "rocks in her head." But the rock also represented Phyllis; how hardened Phyllis felt she needed to be to recover from the trauma of losing her sister; how she lost her sister to a broken neck and then had to watch the bizarre replaying of that death with the horse. The rock was singularly able to bring the emotional representations, or psychic doubles, of Cara and Phyllis together. It became a meeting ground, an external arena, on which Phyllis's continuing involvement was played out.[5]

We use linking objects to re-create the relationship in the external world, to recapture the vitality and the conflict. Linking objects play the song of the relationship. Ironically, they also keep mourners from adapting and moving on with life.

I realize now that I first became interested in these sorts of magical mementos when I was a boy on the island of Cyprus. In my mid-teens, I saw my grandmother open a knapsack I had never seen before. It contained belongings of my dead uncle and newspaper clippings about his mysterious disappearance. My grandmother opened the knapsack, took each item out, touched it and turned it over, sobbed quietly a while before returning the contents to the sack and putting it away. I only saw her go through this performance once but it burned in my memory. For one thing, I prided myself on knowing all the hiding places in that house, but I never could find the knapsack.

I repressed that experience and was not to remember it for many years until patients began bringing me objects that recalled my grandmother's knapsack. I have often thought that this early experience goes a long way toward explaining my fascination with the way we attribute magical qualities to objects in our own everyday world. We use objects to represent our psychological wishes and struggles. For instance, children carry teddy bears and security blankets (technically known as transitional objects) as they get to know themselves and their environments.[6] Other objects have the illusion of absorbing anxiety: rosaries, worry beads, touchstones. Jewelry can patch up our self-esteem, club emblems and insignias absorb our anxiety about belonging. Fetishes absorb anxiety about sexual performance. Linking objects absorb conflicts about loss.

It is important to distinguish between heirlooms and linking objects. In simple grief, a memento is just a memento. An individual whose grief is on track wears an inherited ring without anxiety, feeling no undue compulsion to protect it and no conflict between a desire to see it and a wish to keep it out of sight.

After my father's death, I waived all rights to his estate but I asked my sisters to choose something symbolic of his for me to keep. They made wonderfully thoughtful choices: a diary of his visit to me in the 1960s in which he described the North Carolina mountains, and his citizenship papers from the British when they took the island of Cyprus in 1922. Stamped with his photograph, the document resounds with the turbulent history my native island and family endured. It hangs on a wall in my house and helps nurture my identity and my connection to him.

The difference between mementos and linking objects falls in that hard-to-define area between choice and compulsion. A linking object is psychologically hot as it revives for the mourner some conflict about the loss and what the loss took from him. For instance, in chapter 2, a passage from Lynn Caine described her attachment to her husband's bathrobe: "I knew it was simply a raggedy old robe, but emotionally it was Martin still embracing me, still comforting me." This robe had all the dynamics to develop into a linking object, but Ms. Caine overrode the compulsion. She worked through that aspect of her grief and threw the bathrobe out.

A great many things serve as linking objects. They are often functional items, typically ones that belonged to the lost person or call the loss to mind. The mourner may select them because they recall the milieu in which the loss occurred. These are called last-minute objects. One of my patients kept the stack of records he was putting on the stereo when news of his brother's death arrived.

Certain songs, gestures, or common phrases also serve as

links and are called linking phenomena. Rain began to fall while my patient Tina attended the funeral of her father who had shot himself in the head after a failed love affair. The song "Raindrops Keep Falling on My Head" popped into Tina's mind. She later associated the lyric with the unacceptable wish to have bullets rain on her father's head. She was angry at him for abandoning her twice, once in divorce, once by a willful death. I did not realize at first how apt the song was for Tina until, by chance, I heard it on the radio. The song continues, "crying's not for me," which summed up Tina's unconscious stance that she would not mourn her father.

Even living people can be linking objects. In my experience, this most often occurs in the case of children whose parents are caught in perennial mourning. In some respects, I was a living linking object—or replacement child—for my mother and grandmother. I kept my dead uncle alive for them: I bore his name and carried on his idealized tradition by being a good student with high ambitions. Fortunately, this unconscious role was tolerable and there were many other positive aspects to my relationships with both mother and grandmother so that the role never overwhelmed me.

Linking objects are distinctive because they are generally not used; a watch is never worn, the expensive Nikon camera sits without film. Instead, the item is usually put out of sight. The survivor occasionally takes it out and allows himself to come under its spell. He always knows of its whereabouts, even though he may seemingly ignore it for a considerable period of time.

A linking object is jealously protected because the mourner uses it to keep grief externalized. Externalizing the grief through the use of the linking object gives perennial mourners a sense of control. If something happens to the linking object so that it can no longer absorb the grief, the mourner is deprived of his or her defense and painful emotions can come crashing in. This is what happened to Sarah.

Sarah and Jeff bought a house set deep in the woods and dreamed of raising children who shared their respect for nature. When Sarah had difficulty conceiving, the infertility took a toll on the marriage. Jeff had an affair, which Sarah discovered. She considered leaving him but dismissed such plans when doctors recommended a new operation to resolve her infertility.

After surgery, the couple's optimism soared. They bought a new hammock, a symbol of the family life in their future, and hung it from two large trees next to the house. One day as they lay in the hammock, an angry and bitter fight erupted. After the argument, they made love. The next day, Jeff was killed in an accident at work.

The hammock became magical for Sarah. She could never allow anyone to lie in it. Nevertheless, she would not take it down even in winter or through heavy rainstorms. It was the meeting ground on which she could connect to Jeff; the good and the bad parts of their relationship were stored in its threads. As time passed, the hammock began to rot. Six years after Jeff's death, it fell off the hooks. Seeing the shreds on the ground, Sarah's conflicting feelings about Jeff overflowed. She internalized them, and became depressed. Because she came to see me for her depression, it was some time before I learned about the existence of the hammock and how Sarah had used it to keep at arm's length both her love for Jeff and her rage at his reaction to her infertility.

Thus depression, when it finally came to me, was in fact no stranger, not even a visitor totally unannounced; it had been tapping at my door for decades.

—WILLIAM STYRON

CHAPTER VII

Engulfed Mourners

When Grief Turns to Depression

A young lawyer with a thriving practice, Steve had been a devoted husband and father until he began an uncharacteristic cycle of womanizing. He had an affair with his wife's best friend, then took up with two of his office's secretaries. His colleagues were outraged. His wife left him; his work slipped. Desperate to save his marriage and his job, he entered therapy.

In his first therapy hours, Steve professed to be bewildered. He truly loved his wife and wanted to stay married. On the other hand, he had overwhelming urges to pursue every attractive woman in his path. There were moments, he confessed, when he felt isolated and distanced from his impulsive behavior, almost as if he were an objective observer.

I asked Steve to talk about his childhood. He mentioned that he was the sole surviving child. His only sibling, a younger brother, had died eighteen months earlier in a motorcycle accident. However, Steve quickly assured me that he had recovered from the death. He and his brother had never been close; they were very different temperamentally.

Steve described his brother as a "character," a capricious ladies' man who had never settled down. Steve had always been the dutiful son, the good student, and the model family man. His parents gave lip service to the sort of life Steve's solid achievements represented, but Steve knew that they took vicarious pleasure in his brother's sexual exploits and they nicknamed him "Don Juan."

After the accident, Steve agreed to handle all the funeral arrangements. His parents had one request: that his brother be buried holding his Playboy Club key. When his parents ignored Steve's objections, he honored their wishes. His brother was placed in the coffin, hands folded across his chest, clasping the culture's most prevalent symbol of sexual pursuit.

Steve's therapy moved quickly over the next few weeks. When he described his womanizing as totally out of character, I asked him if he knew anybody who would behave in such a fashion. He began to draw parallels between his behavior and what he disliked about his brother. He discovered that he had identified with the philandering brother out of his age-old rivalry for their parents' affection. He reactivated the conflict and made alive once again his desire to be the favorite son, a common unconscious wish in children competing for parental love.

UNHEALTHY IDENTIFICATIONS

In the hours after death, we sometimes notice a mourner making fleeting identifications with the physical traits of the lost person. These identifications can be unhealthy, such as when the mourner adopts the symptoms of the last illness.

For instance, Colin M. Parkes reported a case of a woman whose husband had lost his voice due to a stroke. After his death, his widow could not speak for ten days.[1] However, my concern here is with more established identifications that have become troublesome parts of an individual's psyche.

The concept of unhealthy identifications may seem far-fetched but examples of it abound. This is the dynamic which is at work when the child of an abusing parent becomes an abuser himself. The adult knows intellectually that child abuse is wrong, has sworn never to harm a child, but cannot overcome his confusion about abuse. He made identifications in a household where intrusion and aggression were part and parcel of parenting. Unless he is able to work through those identifications, the cycle repeats, despite the best conscious intentions.[2]

We cannot say with any certainty just what went awry in Steve's case, but let's look at the elements. The brother's death was both sudden and violent, two risk factors. There was another risk factor: unfinished business between them. This was decades-old business to be sure, but it was revived when the parents insisted that the Playboy key be placed in the coffin. Finally, as an envious boy, Steve had at least unconsciously wished his brother dead so that he could get a fair share of his parents' admiration. Logically, Steve never wished his brother dead, but the unconscious does not operate logically. Now, his wish was granted, and he felt guilty for it.

Note the difference here between the psychological scheme of the perennial mourner and the engulfed mourner. The perennial mourner replays the relationship endlessly, keeping the boundaries between him- or herself and the lost other clearly defined. The mourner who makes unhealthy identifications loses those boundaries. In doing the work of mourning, Steve had not been able to retire the rivalry for his parents' affection. He assimilated the rivalry; dividing himself to play both parts. His psyche became the battleground.[3] What Steve disliked about his brother became what he disliked about himself. Had he continued on the same path, Steve would have eventually become depressed.

Steve's therapy moved quickly. We focused narrowly on the unresolved grief for his brother and completed work in four months. In one of our last sessions, Steve described looking at a beautiful woman and trying to talk himself out of approaching her. He hit his chest as if addressing the psychic double of his brother within: "I said, 'leave me alone.' " This was enormously gratifying because it indicated that Steve finally did more than rationally understand the psychic process of identification, he understood experientially the dynamic.

In Steve's case, the unhealthy identification was simple to root out because there was real-world history at work. Sometimes an identification is formed on the basis of a psychic truth or myth. I once had an analytic patient who was extremely cautious.[4] He traced his gingerliness to his early childhood when he underwent radiation treatments for a thymus problem. His overprotective mother worried constantly about his health. She made him wear a hat at all times to shield him from the sun since he was already getting plenty of X rays at the hospital. As his analysis progressed, my patient began to wonder about his thymus problem and the roots of his mother's solicitousness. He made some inquiries and discovered that, in fact, his younger brother had been the ill one! My patient had not suffered from thymus problems but he had genuinely anguished during that period over his mother's neglect. He had lost her to the care of his brother. In a desperate unconscious attempt to win her love, he identified with the brother's illness. To be sick and needy meant winning a mother's love, just as for Steve, being a playboy meant winning his parents' affection.

WHEN GRIEF TURNS TO DEPRESSION

It goes without saying that many factors combine to create depression: some psychological, some physiological, some biochemical, some genetic, and some psychosocial.[5] Here, I focus on depression that stems from an unresolved grief and I call people so afflicted engulfed mourners.

The engulfed mourner has no sense that unresolved grief is the source of his or her problem. Steve honestly believed himself recovered from his brother's death and that the loss had no repercussions. This occurred because he had identified with his brother's psychic double indiscriminately, taking in both its loved and hated aspects, a process known as in toto identification. By contrast, in uncomplicated mourning, identifications are made selectively with aspects that complement and enrich. The evidence of in toto identification will generally be more subtle than it was in Steve's case.

Depression is unexpressed anger turned inward. An engulfed mourner has turned inward the anger felt toward the lost other and the resulting guilt. The central question of the work of mourning—whether we can make peace with the relationship, stop replaying it, and move on—proves excruciating for the engulfed mourner. It becomes a question of whether to live, as it did for literature's most famous engulfed mourner, Shakespeare's Hamlet.

To be, or not to be, that is the question,
Whether 'tis nobler in the mind to suffer
The slings and arrows of outrageous fortune,
Or to take arms against a sea of troubles,
And by opposing, end them.[6]

DREAMS

Often the story lines of engulfed mourners' dreams reflect their internal conflicts: identification with both loved and hated aspects of the lost person. Jason dreamed that he wore a fine suit that properly belonged to his dead brother. When he tried to take it off, he could not. The cloth had embedded in his flesh. Before the dream ended, the cloth/skin began to disintegrate. The story line of this dream reflects the identification with the lost brother and, at the same time, expresses the dreamer's wish to be free of the unhealthy identification. But he cannot. Engulfed mourners are, by definition, depressed; therefore, their dreams deal with their depression. For instance, they may dream of having a debilitating condition, such as cancer. One man dreamed that his leg was gangrenous but doctors could not operate to save it.

WILLIAM STYRON: TRIUMPH OVER DEPRESSION

In 1990, novelist William Styron published *Darkness Visible*, a painstaking and eloquent record of his descent into suicidal depression near the age of sixty.[7] Styron came to attribute this depression to the incompletely mourned loss of his mother when he was a young boy. However, Styron recounts that for years he had no idea that her death so marked him. Through hard work and hard drink, he kept at bay his unresolved and unconscious conflicts about her loss. He married, raised a family, and achieved great literary distinction. But grief will out. His body rebelled against alcohol, thus crumbling one of his principal lines of defense. He became despondent, phobic about illness, and eventually unable to work. Melancholy overtook him, and it was a darkness that nothing could penetrate: not success, not the solace of a happy family, not drug therapy.

One night after nearly committing suicide, he enlisted his family to hospitalize him. In the hospital, he slowly began to untangle the source of his anguish. There is no mystery as to why he could not successfully mourn his mother. He was only eleven at her death, too young to allow a parent to disappear and too young to have the psychological apparatus to grieve fully.

Artists often use their art to work through unconscious conflicts. As Styron points out, his fiction, peopled with depressed and suicidal characters, shows just what demons he battled. He had no conscious awareness of depression, but he knew intuitively how to represent it.

> After I had returned to health and was able to reflect on the past in light of my ordeal, I began to see clearly how depression had clung close to the outer edges of my life for many years. Suicide has been a persistent theme in my books—three of my major characters killed themselves. In rereading, for the first time in years, sequences from my novels—passages where my heroines have lurched down pathways

> toward doom—I was stunned to perceive how accurately I had created the landscape of depression in the minds of these young women.[8]

I would also point to the theme of his novel *Sophie's Choice,* which represents the essential dilemma of the engulfed mourner.[9] In the novel, a Jewish mother remains haunted by a split-second decision she made in Nazi Germany about which of her two children to keep by her side. The other one went to a certain death. It reprises the dynamic of the engulfed: How do you kill part of yourself even to save another part?

Styron's willingness to expose his depression was an act of generosity. An equally great service may be his willingness to name unresolved grief as the source of his problem. He proves that time does not heal all wounds: Even fifty years later, an unresolved loss has power.

Families should stay together. Otherwise things get out of control. My father, you know. I can't even remember what he was like, I mean when he was alive. But ever since, it's Papa here and Papa there, and dreams.

—Marilynne Robinson

CHAPTER VIII

A Death in the Family

How Parents and Children Mourn

Sally was referred to me by her family doctor because she was having trouble getting over the cancer death of her husband, Malcolm, some years earlier. In addition to her own problems, she worried that Malcolm still unduly preoccupied her children. After listening to her story, I readily understood her dilemma. This fellow gave new meaning to the expression "hanging on for dear life."

From the moment he learned his cancer was terminal, Malcolm railed against the unfairness of his life being cut short. Sally remembered vividly trying to relieve his distress, which persisted up until the moment of death. In his last months, Malcolm took out a long-range calender and meticulously charted the family's likely history over the next decade. He wrote a series of letters to be read at every major holiday, birthday, graduation, and anniversary. In these missives, he proposed strategies for the boys' schooling and careers, reminded them of his place in their world, and urged them never to let his memory die. "Think of me today tossing a football out back with you boys while Mother stuffs the turkey," went one Thanksgiving missive.

Malcolm's desire to let his children know what kind of person he was, what principles he stood for and what he held dear, had noble elements to it. Undoubtedly, in the months immediately following the death, these letters were consoling to his family. Unfortunately, they also had the effect of keeping the family stuck in perennial mourning. These letters were laced with what made the loss hot: Malcolm's panic and rage at his death, his need to be immortal, and his inability to surrender control over his boys.

The fact that the missives were dated for holidays only made the matter worse. Holidays and other family occasions are important milestones in mourning; they notarize the death. The more holidays without Dad, the more the reality of his death sinks in. With each passing holiday, one adapts a bit more to the loss. Malcolm's letters kept reopening the grief.

Each family is unique, so any discussion of the implications of loss within a family unit must be general. The same risk factors, as discussed in chapter 4, apply to families as they do to individuals. For instance, just as an individual's capacity to mourn may be overloaded by a series of losses, so may a family's. Just as an individual's sense of self may be shattered when a certain person dies, so may a family's sense of identity and destiny be jeopardized when an important member disappears.

A family's script is written from its shared history, myths, tradition, previous losses, and personal expectations. These are powerful forces, and they conspire to direct a drama that compels each family member, even those who are ill-served by their roles. As we all know by now, how we function in our family of origin may differ greatly from the way we act with others in the world. An individual may be competent in his professional life but be bound by his role of the infantile troublemaker within the family. How well a family is reconstituted after death depends on how difficult the role of the lost member is to fill.

The mourning process requires tailoring the many roles we play in our lives to fit the external reality, including the role assigned to us many years earlier in our families of origin. Let me explain. As we grow, all of us come to understand ourselves as individuals with multifaceted identities. I am a husband, a psychoanalyst, a Turkish American, a father, an avid moviegoer, but I am also a son, a brother, and the person in my family who was destined to serve as my dead uncle's replacement.

There is a term in psychoanalysis called *projective identification.*[1] It refers to instances in which an individual ascribes a part of him- or herself to another person. I sometimes notice that a patient experiences me as a child; a closer look reveals that he has projected his child-self onto me. Many psychoanalysts have described the way such projective identifications work in family systems.[2] One member of the family becomes a reservoir for aspects of another's self. For instance, I once knew an adventuresome man who complained that his son was overly timid. Yet close scrutiny of the family system uncovered that the father had a vested interest in keeping the son this way. As a boy, the father had been withdrawn; he developed his boldness as a defense. With his son's birth, he delegated (or projected) his timid self to his son, although he was not consciously aware of doing so. Thus, he had no interest in seeing his son become more intrepid. When the boy showed signs of daring, the father quickly reminded him of the world's many dangers.

In other projective identifications, a family member is unconsciously delegated to take up an old role. For instance, a mother may decide (unconsciously) that her daughter is the embodiment of a hated sister. She cannot help but compete and deny love to her child in the same way that she did to her sister. A family member may be imbued with positive attributes and be seen as the family savior. (Projective identifications do not always have destructive elements.)

When a family member who received projective identifications disappears, the family dynamics have to be reworked. The survivor must seek out another child or sibling to take up the role, or face taking back the aspect of himself that he had projected onto the lost member.

THE TYPE OF DEATH

The way a family member dies and the way it is handled affects the group's ability to mourn. A sudden or violent death proves among the hardest to mourn, for all the reasons discussed in chapter 4. A suicide, with the implicit guilt, the shame, and the stigma—added to the suddenness and violence—predisposes a family for complicated mourning. Not only is there likely to have been family stress before the suicide, but all members may struggle with guilt over not having done enough to "rescue" the victim.

Children who lose a parent to suicide often believe that they caused the unhappiness or at least are culpable for not assuaging the pain. Comments by the parent such as "you're driving me crazy," take on resonance that may plague a child throughout his or her life. Losing a parent to suicide may also be the basis for suicidal thoughts in the child, thanks to unconscious identifications.

Furthermore, someone choosing to abandon the family incites anger in those left behind. That anger is often repressed because it seems unacceptable to rage at someone who died either violently or by suicide; the victim has been punished enough.

Families that recover best after loss are those with reasonably healthy structures (not an undue amount of projective identifications) and a sturdy sense of family identity. Practically speaking, a tradition of honesty and respect within a family helps in mourning; each family member should be allowed to vent feelings and ask questions. Ideally, facts about the death are shared with each member in an age-appropriate manner, and participation in mourning rituals is encouraged.

WHEN PARENTS LOSE CHILDREN

After the death of his daughter, Sophie, Freud wrote to a friend that to have a child predecease a parent is a monstrous thing.[3] It is the most difficult loss that humans mourn. With the conception of a child, parents unconsciously adjust their sense of the future as something that holds that child. With the death of a child, parents lose not only a precious tie but also a projected future. Thus, the death may be too hot to mourn. Also, children's deaths are often complicated by guilt. As parents, we believe we should somehow protect our children, even when they are beyond our protection.

The death of a child, still dependent and at home, disturbs the equilibrium in the family; if such a loss does not unite a family, it can pull it irreparably apart as members struggle to make sense of the loss and to vent their anger and guilt. I once knew a couple who lost two children in a commercial plane crash. The husband had spent weeks overriding his wife's objections that the preadolescent children were not old enough to fly alone. The accident stemmed from engine problems, but the wife blamed her husband for allowing them to fly and the bond between them was broken.

How do you ever recover from the loss of a child? I'm not sure. As Freud wrote to his friend on the day his daughter would have turned thirty-six, "Although we know that after such a loss the acute state of mourning will subside, we also know we shall remain inconsolable and will never find a substitute. No matter what may fill the gap, even if it be filled completely, it nevertheless remains something else."[4] And actually this is how it should be. It is the only way of perpetuating that love which we do not want to relinquish.

Some parents adaptively channel their grief into organizations that work to prevent other such deaths. For instance, Handgun Control, Inc., was founded by parents whose son was murdered in a random shooting; Mothers Against Drunk Driving enlists parents whose children were killed in alcohol-related car crashes. Anne Blake, whose daughter, Dolores, died of AIDS, decided to help break the conspiracy of silence around AIDS deaths. She speaks to groups about her loss and works as a bereavement counselor at St. Vincent's Hospital in New York City. These are creative responses to suffering.

MOURNING A MISCARRIAGE

One in five pregnancies ends in miscarriage. Yet, as a culture, we are strangely cavalier about such losses. We often do not recognize that the parents had established a deep bond with the unborn child and that they need to mourn that lost bond. Instead, our standard, well-intentioned comments have the effect of diminishing the relationship. We tell the parents how sorry we are, then add that there will be plenty of other children. We suggest that the miscarriage was no doubt a blessing because the fetus may have had birth defects. Miscarriage often stirs a sense of failure and inadequacy in both parents, but particularly in the mother and, if she is not allowed to grieve, she may have long-term difficulties with loss.

LOSING A SIBLING

When I was in my early teens, my family traveled to my father's boyhood village to visit relatives during a village festival. Our hosts were taking part in a play that marked the start of the festivities; costumes and props were strewn all over the house. One day as my sister and I were horsing around, I picked up what I assumed was a prop gun and aimed it at her head. Our host shrieked at me that the gun was loaded. Horrified, I dropped it.

This memory faded through the years. In the 1980s, my sister visited me in Virginia. While there, she was diagnosed as having a brain tumor and was admitted to the University of Virginia Hospital. Shortly before her surgery, I had occasion to have a massage. The masseuse commented that my right forearm and hand were tensed, and she began intensely kneading the forearm. Guilt rocked through me as I flashed on the memory of my right hand aiming a gun at my sister's head and nearly blowing out her brain. I believe this sensation was impelled by the fact that my sister's brain once again was endangered.

My sister did not die, yet even the threat of losing her was enough to send me into mourning and to heat up my relationship with her psychic double. She lingered in a coma for days, and during that time, she was very much on my mind. I use this story to show how childhood dynamics revive when, as adults, we lose—or have a threatened loss—of a sibling. We unconsciously review all the cycles of childhood.

My profession usually emphasizes the ambivalence in sibling relationships, the so-called sibling rivalry. But clinical studies also show how positive and helpful sibling connections are. For instance, sibling experience teaches us how to share, how to be companionable, how to negotiate with a peer, and how to be responsible. These positive aspects are reviewed after a sibling dies. The conflict also revives. The review inevitably stirs longing, guilt, or anger toward the sibling, which may be muted and tolerable, or upsetting.

Finally, the loss of a sibling marks the end of a childhood illusion that we will all grow old together. Too, the death is a harbinger of things to come. "When a sibling dies," noted writer Barbara Ascher after the AIDS death of her brother, "death tugs at our own shirttail. There's no unclasping its persistent grip. 'You too,' it says. 'Yes, even you.'"[5] We mourn the sibling's death and our own.

CHILDREN'S RESPONSES TO LOSS

There is consensus in the field on two points about childhood loss. We know from studying the unconscious that separation, even to a small child, is experienced as a tearing away. Secondly, we know that the more experience a child had with the lost person and the more he or she is able to maintain the psychic double, the closer a child's mourning will be to an adult's.

In order to understand how any given child is likely to react to death, however, there are a number of considerations: the child's age and innate resiliency, the security of the home environment, the type of death, and the ability of the adults to provide substitutes and solace.[6]

But first we must look at a child's ability to understand the concept of death, an understanding that changes according to the child's age.

Prior to age two or three, children who lose important figures in their lives simply sense that something is missing, a sensation not unlike the feeling of being hungry. An adult's grief involves disengaging from the psychic double of the lost other. But a child at this age has little object constancy (the ability to form and maintain the other's psychic double) and so his or her grief does not resemble an adult's. He or she will have the seminal experience of growing up in a single-parent household or growing up in a household with a grieving parent. He will create a fantasy image of the lost person and will attempt to keep this fantasy image.

At age two or three, the child may be able to understand something of the concept of death with adult help, simply because he or she has most likely seen something dead—a bug, a flower, or a pet. One little boy of four accepted the news that his father had gone to heaven with equanimity. Three months later, he was disconsolate when the father missed his preschool play. The boy had assumed heaven was no different than other locations. Children may express an inability to understand death in such comments as "I know you told me that Mommy will not come back, but I want to call her on the phone."

From age five to ten, death is seen as reversible and temporary, leading to a kind of wish/reality in which the child secretly believes the other is not dead. Between ages five and nine, the child knows what death *is* but does not think it can happen to him or her. After age ten, children have a more realistic concept of death and its finality.

A preadolescent child's reactions to loss often look strange to an adult, not at all what we expect of the grief-stricken. A child may exhibit more surface sadness at the death of a pet than she or he does at a family member's death. Grief over the pet's death is manageable, so the child can allow its expression. The death of an important adult may be too threatening to face, so unconsciously the child denies it and shows no signs of sadness. Novelist Bruce Duffy remembers his family thinking that he was unfeeling when he lost his mother at eleven, that he had only a "wild, obnoxious propensity to laugh at inappropriate times."[7] It seems likely that, unconsciously, he could not tolerate sad feelings so he unconsciously changed them to laughter. We call this reversal of affect.

ADOLESCENCE

As discussed earlier, adolescence serves as a psychobiological rehearsal for mourning. The adolescents unconsciously relax their ties to their parents and transfer some allegiance to peers. The successful completion of adolescence leaves an individual with an adult model for mourning.

CONSEQUENCES OF CHILDHOOD LOSS

As a child grows, she or he learns to surmount different fears and fantasies: fear of separation, fear of not being loved, fear of bodily harm, and fear of not living up to one's own expectations. When a dramatic loss occurs, it gets entangled in the child's psyche with the developmental drama under negotiation. The child feels somehow to blame and may either repress or become stuck at that point.

Let us consider the hypothetical case of Abe and discuss his likely response to loss at various ages. These scenarios are intended to show lingering effects of loss at its most severe. They are not intended to suggest that childhood loss necessarily results in problematic lives.

If Abe's mother dies before he can maintain her psychic double at age two, he will later create a fantasy image of her. Without an effective substitute caretaker, he may grow to be an adult who constantly searches out women but cannot stay loyal to any one of them. Or Abe may take the opposite route and become overly dependent and cling to one, most likely older, woman. If the mother's death occurred when Abe was two or three, Abe may grow up feeling that there is something inherently unlovable about him. Defensively, he may develop the sense that he is entitled to everyone's love and attention. If Abe's father dies while Abe is working out Oedipal issues of rivalry between ages three and five, Abe may grow to be someone who struggles with competition. The slightest provocation, such as an impatient remark from a boss, may feel like a challenge. Or Abe could take another route and search constantly for a strong father with whom to identify. In competition, Abe might either become highly aggressive or seek to avoid competing, because the residual Oedipal guilt leads him to experience winning as threatening, beating, or even killing another.

As a child grows, he develops a fantasy image of the absent parent without the tempering real-world experience that children from intact families have of their parents. For instance, a child of six may idealize his mother as being all-loving and powerful. As he grows, his notion of her as a fairy princess mother will be modified, as he begins to see that she has shortcomings and tailors his psychic double appropriately. If the mother dies before he is able to frame her realistically, he will have difficulty finding people who measure up to her.

In general, children who lose a parent before they have completed adolescence—and who do not have good substitutes to replace the parent or help them mourn—will end up as perennial mourners. The parent becomes a "lost immortal" figure—a haunting absence.[8] The child narrator of Marilynne Robinson's *Housekeeping* explained, "My mother left me waiting for her and established in me the habit of waiting and expectation which makes the present moment most significant for what it does not contain."[9] That is what happened to Barbara, who lost her father at age four.

BARBARA

Barbara was four years old when her father died in a plane crash. His job with the FBI required frequent travel, so his death initially made little impact. When her mother told her he was never coming back, Barbara was not old enough to grasp the finality of death. Instead, she began to wish nightly for his return. At that age, a child believes a wish can perform magic. She wished so consistently that her father would return that she grew confident her wish had been granted; the "truth" was that he was alive.

As Barbara grew, she intellectually knew that her father was dead. But her previous wish-reality endured in her unconscious. In that recess, Barbara developed the theory that her father worked undercover. She envisioned him as a modern-day Eliot Ness—a virtuous man who sacrificed the private satisfactions of family life to rid the nation of hoodlums.

Her mother remarried when Barbara was in junior high school. Barbara found her stepfather innocuous enough, but no competition for her hero father. When her mother confided that she would not have any more children, Barbara fleetingly took this as a sign that her mother also knew her father was alive. In the next moment, Barbara dismissed the notion as farfetched.

As a teenager, Barbara showed little of the typical adolescent's preoccupation with rock stars, athletes, and movie stars. Instead, she devoured detective fiction and TV police series. She never connected these enthusiasms to her absent father, whose name was seldom mentioned. Throughout high school and college, Barbara was a model student. After college, she started seeing older married men—investigators, prosecutors, defense lawyers—who spent their days bringing criminals to justice.

At the start of the affairs, Barbara was euphoric: She would tell friends she had lucked into the perfect romance. After four to six months, the affair unraveled as Barbara's mood darkened. She would pick a fight so that the man would leave. Once again alone, Barbara would grow depressed and punishingly self-critical. Within several months, a new "perfect man" would appear and Barbara rebounded. The cycle repeated five times in about four years. Then Barbara met Justin. True to the pattern, Justin was older and married. He kept his work secret and left town suddenly "on assignments," leading Barbara to think he was an undercover agent. In a few months, Barbara grew edgy and couldn't sleep. When she did nod off, her dreams were disturbing. In one, she dreamed of a maternal woman who walked hand-in-hand with a little girl. In her other hand, the woman held the leash of a gentle puppy. The child tried to approach the puppy, and it metamorphosed into a vicious snake.

Justin grew furious when Barbara tried to break with him. He hounded her. One night he broke her door down, in the process bruising and gashing Barbara, who was trying to hold it shut. She was still crying after the emergency room staff stitched her up, and so she was admitted to the psychiatry ward.

When the doctors charted the cycles of highs and lows, they diagnosed Barbara as having a bipolar disorder, known to the layman as manic depression. One of her doctors believed that her father's early death played a part in her problem and called me for a consultation. I agreed, and Barbara began outpatient treatment with a younger colleague under my supervision.

What emerged in psychotherapy was that Barbara's affairs with married men were searches for her father just as surely as her teenage addiction to detective shows had been. Barbara never mourned her father, in part because a four-year-old is incapable of releasing such an important figure without an adequate substitute. Because her father "lived," she could allow no man to replace him. When she became attracted to a man, she would project her fantasy father image onto him—and she was elated to have "found" Daddy. The relationship was inevitably doomed because she would become disillusioned when this perfect man revealed himself to be merely human. At the same time (because the unconscious does not operate logically), the affair caused her to feel guilty because of its incestuous overtones. After all, she was sleeping with Daddy, who properly belonged to Mommy. She was the little girl in the dream who turned her mother's puppy into an ugly snake. When guilt overwhelmed her, she would provoke the final argument and rid herself of the lover. The cycle would be complete: He loved her, she loved him, but they could not be together. She thus would recreate the loved-but-abandoned scenario of her childhood: seeking Daddy, finding him, losing him.

In her psychoanalytic therapy, Barbara transferred many of these feelings to her therapist. She unconsciously invested him with all of the emotions she once projected onto lovers and onto her dead father. Over time, she was able to remember her childhood, interpret and rework it within the therapeutic setting. Thus Barbara slowly began to mourn, giving up her therapist/father. She gradually was able to stop searching for her father in every man she met. She was no longer doomed to repeat the cycle because she had resolved the relationship with her father.

THE IMPORTANCE OF GOOD SUBSTITUTES

It stands to reason that a child with happy family relationships and an innate sense of love and security will best be able to negotiate crisis, including the pain of loss. Anna Freud and Dorothy Burlingham's study of London children during the World War II air raids proves this point. They found that young children with calm and reassuring mothers or mother-substitutes escaped psychological damage: The mothers provided protective environments in which the children felt safe, despite the fact that the world outside was exploding. And the reverse proved true: If the mother was anxious about the bombing, the child was anxious.[10]

As the following story illustrates, a surviving parent's ability to cope—how fully he or she mourns, comforts the child, and provides the child with adequate substitutes—affects the way the child recoups after loss.

JANET

Janet's father was a soldier who died overseas during World War II while she was still an infant. She had no memory of him, only a photograph of him holding her when he was home on furlough. Janet's mother was a perennial mourner.

She moved in with relatives and became obsessed, during the first five years of her daughter's life, with bringing her husband's body home. Her diligence paid off. The husband's casket was interred in the local cemetery. The mother remarried and had another child. With the remarriage and her half-sister's birth, Janet experienced the loss of her mother's individual attention, the loss of the relatives she and her mother had lived with, the loss of her mother to a new sibling. All of these concrete losses merged with the loss of her father.

Janet's mother kept part of herself segregated from her new life. That part was reserved for her unresolved grief and Janet became its standard-bearer. Janet was entrusted with a locked box of the father's letters; on Janet's bedroom wall hung his oversized portrait. Her stepfather wanted to adopt Janet so that she would have the same name as the rest of the household, but her mother forbade it.

Memorial Day celebrations in her small hometown left Janet feeling at once special and forlorn. The daughter of the town's only war casualty, Janet was designated to put a flag on a small monument that bore her father's name.

Her mother imparted to Janet the sense that the world was rife with loss and calamity. When Janet flew to Washington, D.C., and a plane crashed in California, her mother took it as an omen. She paced nervously until Janet telephoned, and then she confided frantically what a brush they had with disaster. Contrast this sort of mothering, and the likely effect on a child, with the mothers in wartime London whose reassuring sense of the world was enough to instill calm in their children.

When the Vietnam War wound down, Janet was in her late twenties. Television news footage of the freed prisoners triggered Janet's grief for the father who would never come home to her. Other war-related sights—war films, the Vietnam memorial, Memorial Day celebrations—upset her. At such times, she felt that no one understood the loneliness of being raised without a father.

As an adult, Janet married a much older man. To some extent, she knew this choice was a search for a father substitute. This, in itself, is no indication of disturbance. Whom we choose to love and marry is always influenced by our past relationships. However, Janet fit the pattern of an individual with unresolved childhood losses. She needed to keep a certain distance in her marriage in order to avoid disappointment and abandonment. When she most needed closeness from her husband, she would push him away. She could not acknowledge her dependency since she unconsciously feared another rejection.

Janet generously suggested that I use her story in this book to illustrate the way unresolved grief impairs the ability to connect. However, Janet supplied a happy ending to her tale. In December 1991, she joined in a memorial service at Arlington Cemetery with six hundred others who had lost parents in World War II. This was the long overdue ceremony for her father and it provided Janet with an outlet for her pent-up grief. She met and was able to trade stories with other people who had never known their fathers, thus easing some of her sense of isolation. She ended the day with a sense of peace.

IDENTIFICATION AFTER A PARENT'S DEATH

Ideally, children have two parents with whom they can form identifications that help them grow and negotiate various developmental steps. If a parent is not available, the child unconsciously creates a phantom parent to help him or her negotiate an issue. For instance, a fatherless boy needs to create a rival for his mother in order to resolve the Oedipal drama by which a boy gradually renounces his mother and identifies with his father. The downside to such phantoms is that they are not subject to reality checks, as a present father or mother is. Therefore, these fantasized parents can often be exaggerated, either idealized or made more frightening.

Anna Freud wrote of individuals who are "chronic losers," whose symptom is the inability to keep track of belongings. They continuously mislay their money, forget their homework at school, leave articles of clothing behind when they are visiting friends. She noted two layers of identifications are at work in such cases. Chronic losers identify passively with the lost items (and so refuel their sense of being lost) and they identify actively with their dead parents who left their children behind. Chronic losers treat their possessions as their parents treated them.[11]

Anna Freud's description of chronic losers brings to mind a paper about the children of Israeli soldiers pronounced missing in action. These children repeatedly lost their possessions and complained loudly and tearfully about the losses. When the possessions were found, the children carried them about on display and urged adults in the family to rejoice over the recovery.[12]

Sometimes identifications become more skewed and may reveal themselves as an unusual behavior or characteristic in the surviving child. Nineteenth-century French author George Sand's father died in a riding accident when Sand was four. Psychoanalyst Helene Deutsch believes that Sand's use of a male name, wearing of trousers, and adoption of other habits considered masculine were an identification with him. Sand's many affairs, Deutsch concluded, were a search for a "strong, powerful, god-like father who could restore her femininity" and Sand herself would seemingly have agreed with this conclusion. "I have always felt my infidelities were caused by fate . . . by a search for an ideal which impelled me to abandon the imperfect in favor of what appeared to be nearer perfection."[13]

It is difficult to generalize about human response to trauma, however, or to predict the resiliency of human nature. We would surely have expected disturbance in Fuat, an eighteen-year-old Palestinian youth I met in February 1990 while working on this book. Yet he was able to make healing and enriching identifications. As such, he represents a triumph of the human spirit.

I met Fuat in a school for war orphans in Tunis. At the age of five, he had witnessed the brutal murder of his parents and sisters by enemy soldiers. He was raised in a succession of orphanages in different countries. Over the years, he lost all trace of his roots. He had no heirlooms or photographs and only the haziest memories. When I examined him, he could not consciously recall what his parents looked like. He did have a memory of an accident that occurred when he was about three, and he believes that his parents were present. He ran pell-mell into his grandmother as she cooked sweets on an open fire. Boiling oil splashed up and seared his right leg. He likes to imagine how his parents responded. He is confident, although he has no memory of it, that his father scooped him up and smeared ointment on the burn to soothe the pain. The consequence of that accident is a long, red scar that has become his contact to his family. It represents to him his parents giving him succor and strength. "I keep my parents under my skin," he said to me, touching his leg in a ritual gesture he performs every night before he settles down to sleep. The boy is captain of the orphanage soccer team and is renowned for the sturdy right leg which he uses to power the ball into the goal.

PART THREE

Resolutions

The end of all our exploring will be to arrive where we started and to know the place for the first time.

—T. S. Eliot

CHAPTER IX

Adaptations and Therapy

Most mourners do not need professional help with grief and, in fact, most do not seek it. Most people simply need a supportive social network in which they feel free to express a range of emotions. Generally, a person will be reassured to learn that transient feelings of denial, splitting, bargaining, guilt, and anger are commonplace, to know that the work of mourning is both frustrating and a period of tumult, and to be reassured that routine grief sometimes looks bizarre. Several months after his father's death, a young lawyer dreamed about his father's body blackening and the flesh coming off the bones. The dream horrified him until he went to a bereavement counselor and learned the dream was typical of the sort experienced by people at the end of crisis grief.

As a society, we can help mourners by removing the taboos against talking of death. We can encourage them to speak frankly with relatives and friends of the experience and its accompanying emotions. Most clergy know a good deal about the course of uncomplicated grief. Their ministry with families of the terminally ill, and their experience in overseeing burial rituals, make them sensitive to mourners' needs to vent ambivalence, pain, and anger. Those with no religious affiliation usually create their own rituals to mark this drastic passage in their lives. For example, they choose a significant spot to spread a loved one's ashes or otherwise creatively memorialize him or her. Programs such as Widow-to-Widow or Compassionate Friends have proved enormously helpful by offering grievers the opportunity to meet with others who have suffered similar losses. These support groups offer a safe setting in which a mourner can dissipate guilt and anger.

The early chapters of this book should be a source for caregivers and bereavement counselors in devising a helpful therapeutic attitude. For instance, the widower of a heart attack victim who complains of chest pains, yet has no underlying physical symptoms, may be displaying the beginning of an unhealthy identification. He should be monitored with that in mind.

Work with individuals who lost parents at puberty has shown us that adolescent mourners should not be "spared," but should be encouraged to express their grief and participate in funeral rites. Those who have gone through adolescence can grieve like adults. Children's reactions to death differ according to age, as noted in the previous chapter. However, even a young child needs to know that grief is an experience that can have a beginning and an end. It is important for the child to see that the adults involved grieve and then move beyond grief.

For the relatively small number of people who require psychotherapeutic help to resolve conflicts stirred by loss, treatments range from brief psychotherapy to psychoanalysis. In order to be effective, such therapy will take the time to explore what the loss means to the individual and how mourning became complicated. Unfortunately, the current vogue in psychiatry is to prescribe drugs, so medication is replacing substantive treatment. This reliance on medication is driven by economic pressures and the fact that insurance carriers are reluctant to cover anything more than a quick-fix therapy. It is wrongheaded to use drugs on an individual suffering from complicated grief. The anecdotes in this book underscore the importance of unlocking emotion in order to resolve mourning. Drugs muffle emotions; they impair the course of mourning.

BRIEF PSYCHOTHERAPY

My favorite brief psychotherapy experience concerns a gentle middle-aged woman I will call Louise. Her family doctor believed she was paranoid and psychotic. Knowing that her symptoms began after her son's death, he sent her to me. When I first met Louise and her husband in my waiting room, their distress was palpable. They held hands tightly. I took Louise into my office and she quickly exploded about getting to the bottom of "the foul play."

Once she calmed down, Louise told me the following story. She had two married sons; the younger had died recently while piloting his private airplane. His wife had been in the airplane with him, yet escaped without injury. My patient maintained that her daughter-in-law had engineered the accident, even though aviation authorities found the accident resulted from her son's carelessness. This was not the only misdeed Louise attributed to her daughter-in-law. Louise had suspected that the young widow had been trying to poison her husband in the weeks before the accident.

By the time I saw her, Louise had spent a year, and much of her energy, trying to get to the bottom of the accident.

She hired a detective to investigate her daughter-in-law and to review autopsy and accident reports. She reported lying awake nights trying to solve the mystery. Her sleepless state merely fueled her suspicions. Louise's husband tried to convince her that the daughter-in-law was unlikely to have plotted their son's murder since the marriage had been a happy one. Furthermore, had the daughter-in-law wanted the airplane to crash, she would not have plotted the accident to occur when she was a passenger.

During our initial interview, Louise freely discussed her theory of foul play. As she spoke, I began to realize that her son's death reactivated some past conflicts about loss, and that Louise herself was once the victim of "foul play."

Louise was a middle child and the only girl in a large family. Her childhood had been dominated by boys, but her parents' kindness made it bearable. When she was thirteen, one of her brothers died from a ruptured appendix. Louise's mother became a perennial mourner, obsessed with the dead boy. As the only girl, Louise became responsible for running the house and caring for her brothers. No one paid attention to her; when she graduated from high school, the family did not even show up for the graduation.

Thus, Louise saw herself as getting the short end of the stick, the victim of foul play. (Even the sports terminology reflects that her childhood was dominated by boys.) Her adaptation was to become a do-gooder. She went to work after graduation and throughout her early twenties, put aside most of her checks to help pay for an operation for another of her brothers. She met and married an undemanding man who gave her the mothering she had missed. They had two sons. Her unselfish, "others first" life-style persisted. She used it as a defense to keep from facing her anger at her mother's neglect.

One day, Louise's mother decided that she was near death. She summoned her now adult children and confided in them that she had for years safeguarded certain "secret objects" belonging to her dead son. Her "dying" request was that her children and their children guard these linking objects with their lives. Louise was outraged, although she said nothing. As her mother lingered, Louise realized how much of her teen years had been lost and how her mother had indulged her own grief at the expense of Louise's happiness.

As Louise recited her suspicions and complaints about her daughter-in-law, she referred repeatedly to how "uncaring" the daughter-in-law had seemed during her husband's funeral. It became clear to me that Louise linked the coldness of the two women in the face of sorrow and suffering. I asked Louise to consider the connection between the "uncaring" daughter-in-law and "uncaring" mother. I suggested that the sedatives prescribed for the daughter-in-law may have made the younger woman appear insensitive. Louise left the session wondering whether she had judged her daughter-in-law unfairly. On the way home from that first session, she stopped by her daughter-in-law's house. The two women stayed up all night talking and weeping together over their common loss. Louise began to see the younger woman as a deeply caring widow. She no longer insisted on casting her as a younger version of her mother and was able to separate the two experiences. This revelation began to put her grief back on course.

Over the next six months, I saw Louise eight times. In one of her earliest sessions, she spontaneously reported a childhood memory that was connected to the theme of foul play. When Louise was about thirteen, her brother (the one who would be dead a few months later) had been teasing her. To retaliate, she hurtled his prize toy airplane down the stairs, where it smashed into small pieces. This memory and the accompanying guilt had been repressed in her for years.

Louise's treatment in the remaining sessions centered on the childhood loss of her brother and the unconscious guilt provoked by his death. Her ability to grieve for her brother was impaired because his death carried the subsidiary loss of her mother's love and attention.

The death of Louise's son revived her childhood guilt. However, this guilt, in all its implications, was too much for her to acknowledge consciously. The basic scenario remained intact: A woman was responsible for an airplane crash and a man's subsequent death, but through projective identifications, she assigned the "murderer" role to her daughter-in-law.

Because Louise came to see me only for brief psychotherapy, we did not explore other issues raised by her story, nor did we attempt to change her basic character structure. Bringing her guilt about the deaths and her anger with her mother to the surface was enough to start her on a normal course of mourning. She then experienced normal grief and remained symptom-free. She wrote to me after the second anniversary of her son's death. At this anniversary, her whole family, including her son's widow, had a ceremony to honor the dead man. This memorialization marked the end of the work of mourning, and she no longer needed my services. For a few years more, I received Christmas cards from Louise, who seemed to be doing well.

REGRIEF THERAPY

When I arrived at the University of Virginia Medical Center in 1963 as a young instructor in psychiatry, I was given for an office a windowless room that was the size of a closet. Since I was excited to be a member of a distinguished faculty, and sanguine about being on the bottom of the totem pole in the department, I willingly accepted the location. This closet was next to the many-windowed corner office occupied by Dr. Joseph Wolpe, one of the stars of that era, who was attracting a great deal of attention for his work in behavioral therapy. Behaviorists believe that all psychological problems stem, not from unconscious conflicts, but from learned responses and conditioning.

Meanwhile, I had applied to the Washington Psychoanalytic Institute to begin a training analysis and education at the behest of my mentor, psychoanalyst Dr. David Wilfred Abse. Once accepted, I undertook the trip to Washington several times a week, even though in those days the round-trip drive was nearly six hours. My commitment to psychoanalysis made my position in the department a bit uncomfortable. Our chairman made a point of inserting comments at weekly faculty meetings that psychoanalysis would be a dead profession in twenty years. Then there was the success of Dr. Wolpe, whose long waiting list of patients hoping to be "deconditioned" was hard to ignore.

Wolpe often pointed at the ineffectiveness of psychoanalysis when he could "cure" people quickly. Looking back, I think I was envious of him and admired his confidence even though he did not believe in the unconscious, the cornerstone of psychoanalysis. In simplest terms, Wolpe believed that if a man was phobic about dogs, it stemmed from a frightening experience with dogs in his past, whereas my training led me to believe that, yes, the fellow was frightened of dogs, but it was at least worth exploring whether the animal represented other unconscious and repressed fears.

I suspect my fellow analysts would say that my wish to find a way to decondition patients as Wolpe did originated in "identification with the aggressor" or, in this case, my growing rivalry with him. But, unlike Wolpe, I did not want to decondition people from external fears, such as dogs or spiders, but to decondition them from internal fears. I decided that individuals who had problems with grief would be ideal candidates for such narrow therapy. Why not, I thought, develop a method to decondition mourners against the conflict stirred by loss?

Thus, I devised a crude method of treatment called regrief therapy, which largely ignored an individual's general psychological being and focused narrowly on reactions to a concrete loss.[1] I began to seek out patients who were aware of being stuck in grief. I fixed solely on the lost relationships, their memories of the dead, their reactions to the precise moments of the death, their response to the funeral, and so forth. It astounds me now to recall how mechanistic and interventionist I was in those days, continually trying to sort out the distortions in their thinking and misplaced guilt.

Spurred by my work with Alice, who used scrapbooks and photographs to help review her life with her grandfather, I began to ask mourners to bring in photographs of the dead persons. I thought that looking at a picture and talking about the deceased would help the survivor speak frankly about just who the dead person was and what he or she had meant. All this was an attempt to tame the dead person's influence and to decondition the patient so that he or she would not spend years trying to fight old battles.

A funny thing happened. Along with the photographs, some patients brought in possessions and other objects that they felt conveyed some psychic truth about the lost relationships. Sometimes they would bring in objects to which they would profess mild indifference. At other times touching or even looking at these same objects elicited waves of guilt, fear, pain, or even rage. Initially, I was rather bewildered at the responses and wondered what I had unleashed. Soon, however, their visceral reactions to these broken watches, banged-up cameras, and cracked eyeglasses recalled my grandmother's hidden knapsack of her dead son's belongings and made me "discover" linking objects.

As I developed professionally, I grew disenchanted with the idea of magical cures. Nevertheless, I stayed with the term regrief therapy. This evolved as a way to determine at what point a mourner's grief became stuck, to loosen that fixation, and to allow the mourner to "regrieve" the loss from that point. Over the years, the therapy became less rigid, and I spent more time exploring what alarms loss set off in the mourner. Linking objects remained the focus of the treatment.

Regrief therapy generally takes two to four months, during which time the patient is seen three to four times a week. Given the nature of the material confronted, this means that the treatment is quite intense. Regrief candidates must be selected with care. They must have sufficient psychological strength to endure the anxiety evoked by the process. The most suitable patients for regrief are those perennial mourners who live with an active hope to see the lost persons again, but still dread the reunions because reunions imply that the mourning will never resolve. The dynamics of the engulfed mourning and perennial mourning can overlap in some cases; if the depression is not rigidly fixed, such candidates can successfully regrieve. I believe firmly that regrief should be tried only once. If the first treatment is not successful, another psychotherapy, one that focuses on a major psychological change, is indicated.

REGRIEF: AN OVERVIEW

First, the therapist conducts a diagnostic interview to identify the reasons the patient is unable to mourn, taking into account childhood developmental losses as well as concrete losses. I also try to discern whether there is an introject or any unhealthy identifications and to pinpoint the linking object, without revealing my formulations to the patient.

Since the patient is preoccupied with the lost other, one of the first goals of regrief therapy is to help the patient distinguish between her- or himself and the lost person. For example, a patient spoke of a scathing letter he had received from his father shortly before the father's death. Later in the session, the patient began criticizing himself in an unconscious echo of his father's words. I pointed out the similarities between the comments and asked him to differentiate his feelings from those of his father's. This approach begins to untangle the tie between the mourner and the lost other. Paradoxically, it also stirs up emotion, guilt, anger, and sadness, as the fact of the death becomes more real.

I then encourage the patient to speak of the loss, to recall the circumstances of the final illness or accident, to discuss his or her reactions to seeing the corpse and attending the funeral. In doing so, I am guided by my formulation of how the grief complicated. I avoid questioning the patient directly, instead I attempt to guide him or her to insight through the use of interpretation and clarification.

Eventually, the patient realizes that one side of his or her ambivalence—the longing to recover the lost relationship—is counterbalanced by eagerness to be out of its thrall. Rather than reassuring the patient that such ambivalence is normal, a therapist conveys that message through therapeutic neutrality and empathy. These empathetic remarks lead the patient to examine why he or she alternately wants to "save" and "get rid of" the lost other. Around this point, the patient grows angry and in other ways relives past experiences connected with the death and the dead. The patient has begun to regrieve.

After a sufficient amount of emotion is vented, I ask the patient to bring a linking object to a session. At first, the patient ignores the object's presence. Eventually, he or she is asked to touch it and to report what comes to mind. The patient generally likens the linking object to a magic box in which a conflicted relationship is stored. I never fail to be impressed with the intense emotion that is invested in the linking object, and I would caution other psychotherapists about it. A linking object can touch off emotional storms that continue for weeks. Diffuse at first, they later become differentiated, allowing therapist and patient to sort out feelings of anger, guilt, remorse, sadness, and so on. The linking object then begins to lose its power, whether or not the patient chooses to discard it.

As the linking object loses potency, the patient grows somber and is ready to complete mourning. Patients take final steps as if to say goodbye to the relationship, such as visiting a grave (if they have never done so) or devising some other way to commemorate the loss.

Throughout the process, dreams provide a clue to where the patient is in regrief. My patient Kelly dreamed of a green field at the start of his therapy. In subsequent dreams, the field was plowed up for a narrow ditch, then the dead father appeared alive but wheelchair-bound. In one of the last dreams, Kelly put his father and the wheelchair into the ditch. In a week or so, he told me that he once again dreamed of a clear green field. "But this time," he said, "I know my father is under the green grass, dead and buried." This signaled the end of his regrief work.

JULIA: A CASE OF REGRIEF

Julia, a single woman in her early thirties, worked as a secretary. She came to our psychiatric unit because she had trouble sleeping, was feeling hopeless and unable to summon any interest in her job. Her mother had died seven months earlier, and Julia had ever since been plagued by a sense that her mother was perhaps not really dead and was watching her every move and might come back. At night, Julia had disturbing dreams in which her mother made various attempts to return to life. In one particularly frightening dream, Julia's mother was banging furiously on her coffin, trying to get out, while Julia begged the mortician to administer a large dose of a tranquilizer. These dreams became so terrifying to her that we made the decision to hospitalize her.

I liked Julia immediately. When she was not panicked about her mother's imminent return, she was personable and highly intelligent. She gave me a cohesive personal history. The more we spoke, the more sure I was that she would be a good candidate for regrief therapy. I arranged to see her four times a week during her hospitalization. The nurses who cared for her also had some training in regrief work and were sensitive to its course. She received no drugs.

Julia had already demonstrated that she saw her mother ambivalently, even though she would have shrunk from that description. In the diagnostic interview, Julia described her mother alternately as a "monster" and "a very sweet person."

Julia had lived at home with her parents all of her life. When Julia's father died, the five older siblings left home and, for ten years, Julia devoted herself to the care of her invalid mother, a diabetic who was wheelchair-bound because of a leg amputation.

I suspected that her problems separating from her mother in death were related not only to her slavish devotion to her for the last decade but to Julia's early history. When Julia was only six months old, her mother was badly burned in a fire and was unable to care for Julia for nearly a year. I began with the premise that this early disruption of the mother-child unit made Julia sensitive to separations and approval. This need to feel connected, I theorized, played out in their later relationship and in Julia's difficulty in letting her mother go.

In her initial sessions, I asked Julia to tell me about her relationship with her mother. The mother required servitude; she undermined and derided Julia. Julia took the abuse because she had grown up with the idea that she and her mother had a "special bond."

When I visited her hospital room during the first week of

therapy, I found Julia lying in bed stiffly. "Look at me, I am like a corpse," she said. She was upset over the flowers in her room because they made it look "like a funeral parlor." Sometimes she complained of weakness in her legs and difficulty in walking. It was hard to miss these attempts to destructively identify with her dead mother who in life had been unable to walk. I explained to her that her symptoms belonged to her mother. I suggested that these confused identifications might be related to her guilt about her wish to be free of the mother's tyranny.

Julia began to speak more openly than before about her mother's oppressive demands and the sacrifices Julia had made in her name. She had given up the chance to go to college, and broken up with her boyfriend when he asked her to move with him to another city. She admitted that on occasion she had wished her mother dead. These rebellious thoughts made her feel so guilty that she redoubled her service to the old woman. She began calling her mother from work several times a day and sleeping at the foot of her bed "to make sure she kept breathing."

However, a year before the mother's death, Julia did something uncharacteristically independent. She contacted the old boyfriend and arranged to spend a week with him. During the trip, she bought a red nightgown. When she returned from her trip, her mother saw the nightgown and demanded it. The mother wore it almost continually for the next year, and died in it. In one of Julia's "hallucinations," her mother appeared in her hospital room wearing the red nightgown.

After Julia told me this history, I asked her to consider that she had reason to feel ambivalently about her mother, and I expressed the hope that our therapy would help her recognize some of these issues.

I learned that Julia's family perpetuated the idea that she and her mother had a special bond. They "protected" her from seeing her mother's body and moved quickly into the house and removed all reminders of her mother's death. Julia managed secretly to retrieve the red nightgown, which she threw into a garbage bag, tied tightly, and tossed into the back of a closet. When I heard this detail, I knew that the red nightgown was a linking object.

At the funeral, the minister singled out Julia, praising her devotion to her mother and celebrating her sacrifices. This sermon made Julia feel like a fraud and hypocrite. "If only they knew how many times I wished her dead!" Julia said. At the end of the service, she approached the open coffin to look at her mother's corpse, but fainted before she got a glimpse. Thus, Julia's fears that her mother could return were enabled by the fact that Julia never saw her corpse.

A few weeks into our work, the theme of Julia's dreams centered on running away and trying to escape from the powerful, vindictive mother. The unit nurses noted Julia's cheerful facade had been dropped, and she seemed solemn. At this time, I asked a relative to retrieve the bag holding the red nightgown and bring it to the hospital.

When I arrived in Julia's room for our twelfth session, she gestured toward the garbage bag. When I saw how the neck of the bag was twisted, I could only imagine that poor woman wringing it tightly, as she must have wanted to wring her mother's neck on more than one occasion. Julia would have no part of the bag that day, but her mother's presence was palpable nonetheless. I told her that our goal was to have her be able to open the bag, remove the nightgown, and talk about its meaning, but that she did not need to do this until she felt ready.

Julia finally felt ready to open the bag in a later session. But when she removed the nightgown she panicked; she dropped it and fled the room, screaming "Let me out of here! I can't stand it!" Eventually Julia could stay in the room with the nightgown and use it to connect with memories of her relationship with her mother. Thus, she began to do the review necessary to the work of mourning. I was there to keep her from becoming overly guilty, angry, or sad.

Julia's "hallucinations" disappeared and her dreams about her mother changed once more. Her mother now appeared in them shrunken and small and no longer powerful; in one of them she was floating in a tiny casket. Julia's nurses observed that she seemed to be getting "worse" at this time; she appeared to be more anxious. In fact, my experience has shown that this was a good sign. She was shedding defenses, and feeling appropriately anxious over her loss.

A month into her treatment, Julia's dreams began reflecting her willingness to let her mother go. She dreamed of being at the cemetery for her mother's funeral, but there was no grave—which caused considerable disappointment to the mourners and to her mother, who stood among them. The next night, she dreamed she was pushing her mother in a wheelchair near a cliff. Suddenly she pushed her off. Her mother went without protest, and Julia sensed that it was all right to have done so. In her waking life, her anxiety subsided.

Shortly before her discharge from the hospital, she began showing signs of renewed energy and interest that are characteristic of an individual who is ending mourning. She spoke of the possibility of resuming her relationship with her former suitor. One of her relatives had brought a picture of her mother's grave to her and Julia began looking at catalogues for tombstones.

Two sessions later, I was surprised to hear her account of a ceremony she had organized the day before. She had assembled some fellow patients and ritualistically burned the red nightgown. I had never indicated that she should get rid of the nightgown, much less burn it. However, I did think that her decision to set fire to it resonated with her childhood trauma of losing her mother to fire. The legacy of her mother's absence after that fire set up their difficult relationship and Julia's subsequent problems with separation. By burning the nightgown, Julia was symbolically ridding herself of the unwanted aspects of her relationship with her mother. I learned in the same session that she had ordered a tombstone for her mother's grave. The last thing Julia did before her discharge was to visit the cemetery.

I had a three-year follow-up with Julia through the mail after the completion of her regrief therapy. In one letter she wrote, "I am simply feeling wonderful. I am no longer afraid of the dark, of being alone, of expressing my true feelings." In a wry reference to the burning that had played such a part in her life, she added: "I feel most energetic and have a *burning* [she underlined the word] desire to go places and do things."

Suffering can be productive. We know that painful experiences of all kinds sometimes stimulate sublimations, or even bring out quite new gifts in some people, who may take to painting, writing or other productive activities under the stress of frustrations and hardships. Others become more productive in a different way—more capable of appreciating people and things, more tolerant in their relationships to others—they become wiser.

—MELANIE KLEIN

CHAPTER X

Creative Resolutions

When Grief Inspires

A few years ago, an art gallery in Washington, D. C., sponsored a group show called Memento Mori dealing with death as an inspiration for artists.

One of the exhibits was a large-scale painting titled *Sleeping Beauty,* which depicted a young sailor who died at sea in 1842 and whose body was exhumed in the late 1980s on an island off Canada. Buried under permafrost, the corpse was perfectly preserved—even the eyes were intact. The work is indeed compelling, but equally arresting to me was the study of how Judy Jashinsky came to paint this young sailor. Her story represents an artist's creative adaptation to grief.

Jashinsky lost her father in a trucking accident when she was twelve. He had been a charming but restless man who never settled down. He moved the family every seven or eight months and had them living hand-to-mouth. As the eldest and only girl, Jashinsky was his favorite child. She remembers the thrill of traveling the highways on weekend trips, sitting in the truck cab next to her handsome father. He left one night on a trip with a promise to return in a few days to take the family to Milwaukee on vacation. The family's bags were packed and waiting in the front hall when they learned he had been killed. The injuries were so severe that Jashinsky never saw his body. He left no insurance, no savings, no money to cover the next month's car payment. There were times throughout the next twenty years when Jashinsky would dream that he was not dead at all. "That he had just left, it had all been a set-up. I'd dream that my mother would call us downstairs as we were getting ready for school in the morning and he would be there, or that I'd see him someplace and he would try to hide to avoid me," she recalled.

He became a hero in the household. His portrait sat on the television set "which was the closest thing we had to a shrine in the house," she recalls. His name was rarely mentioned. "When it was, the tone was reverential," she remembers. There was never a whisper of reproach or a hint that his life-style had been less than responsible. The family's canonization of him extended to the anniversary of his death, which they treated "like Good Friday."

Jashinsky came to realize that there were some small benefits to his absence. The family no longer moved frequently. Furthermore, Jashinsky, who had begun to paint in high school, was eligible for full college scholarships. By the time

Jashinsky reached adulthood, she believed that she was free from the traces of his loss. She married a college classmate and embarked on a career in art.

At thirty-seven, she went into psychotherapy, ostensibly because she felt her painting was stagnating and that she was not taking enough risks with her work. "Up to that point, I had done very controlled formal paintings of still-life objects, with a certain compulsiveness to fill in every space on the canvas. If I did paint a figure, it tended to be not fully realized or in the background. I was fighting the responsibility of depicting a fully realized figure," she says.

Jashinsky's problems in her work reflected the dilemma of her unresolved grief. She could only paint hazy, unrealized figures or formal, controlled still lifes that suggest the perennial mourner's sense of being frozen in grief and preoccupied by those who are not fully alive. Of course, at the time she was not aware of what motivated her choice of subjects. In this way, art is like our dreams, working out our unconscious struggles.

Jashinsky's therapist quickly focused her on the loss of her father. She asked Jashinsky to consider her anger at him for leaving the family in the lurch, her unconscious denial that he was dead, and her guilty realization that his death had provided her with an opportunity to go to college. After several months in treatment, her therapist suggested that she write her father a letter to express her feelings about him. Jashinsky went to a favorite spot in Washington's National Gallery and composed it. In it, she told him about how her life had turned out: She described her work and confessed her guilty belief that his death had provided her with opportunities that he could never have given her in life, "so that I had an obligation to make the most of my life and my career." She also vented her anger in two pages full of reproach for his irresponsible life-style. She felt purged and thought she had dealt with her father's death.

The next morning, Jashinsky turned on the "Today" show and was struck by a segment on the perfectly preserved corpse of the young English sailor, John Torrington. "I had never seen my father's body and suddenly, in the midst of dealing with him, I see this corpse," she says. She got a photograph of the body and began to research the history of Torrington's expedition as well as the anthropologist's exhumation of his body. All of a sudden, she realized she was going to paint this young sailor.

She could not face the implications of it, although she remembers tossing it off as a joke to her therapist. "God, after all this, now I'm going to go back and paint a corpse."

I can only admire the creative way Jashinsky expanded on her therapist's instruction to write to her father. She used the letter to initiate a review of her relationship with him and then seized on the story of Torrington, a long-dead young man whose body looked as if the death was yesterday. Torrington was the perfect vehicle for her to resolve her grief for her father, whose loss had been frozen in her mind as if the death had just happened. Jashinsky's account of the evolution of *Sleeping Beauty* corresponds to a textbook description of the way a work of mourning unfolds.

Jashinsky painted the main life-size figure of Torrington in a monthlong rush of creativity. Over the next five months, she filled in details. The painting sat for about sixteen weeks while she tried to ignore a nagging sense that it was not a completed work. Finally, she decided to add side panels to the painting and make it more ceremonial. She painted in leaves, water, smoke, fire. It took another year. She named it *Sleeping Beauty*, and she noticed that she no longer had the recurring dreams of her father. She had dealt not only with her problems with his death, but also with her inability to paint figures, to depict life. "I knew instinctively that it was the best painting I had ever done."

LINKS BETWEEN MOURNING AND CREATIVITY

Artists draw on their unconscious in their work, so it is not surprising that loss frequently fuels creativity. The link between mourning and creativity has always fascinated psychoanalysts, most notably George Pollock and William Niederland, as well as art and literary critics.[1] For the critic, all that counts in a work of art is its aesthetic validity. For the student of mourning, it is interesting to note that a creative work can represent many aspects of mourning: an expression of the artist's continuing conflict over a loss, a creative linking object, an attempt to repair or triumph over grief.

I think of poet Sylvia Plath, who committed suicide and whose poetry often concerned her anguish over her early loss of her father: "At twenty I tried to die/And get back, back, back to you./I thought even the bones would do," she wrote in a poem titled "Daddy."[2] Talent is the determining factor here; Plath's creative work stands as a successful entity, even if the grief never resolves. The literary critic is content; the psychoanalyst is not.

My friend, psychiatrist Demetrios A. Julius, has extensively studied the arrested mourning of John Lennon and the late Beatle's recurring references to his grief in his music.[3] His parents, Alfred and Julia, had met and married as adolescents, but Alfred disappeared periodically after John's birth.

Julia shuttled young John back and forth between her parents and her sisters. When John was five years old, Alfred reappeared and the boy was asked to choose between his parents. He chose his father, but when his mother turned and walked away, John went screaming after her. (He would not see his father again until he was world-famous as a Beatle.) Even after this display of loyalty, his mother left John once again with her sister. The boy became fond of his uncle by marriage, who served as a father figure for him, but the fellow died when John was thirteen. Julia reentered his life in adolescence, and he began to rely on her to the exclusion of all others, including peers. When John was about eighteen, his mother was killed by a car in the street in front of John's house. Julius traces Lennon's loss of his mother, Julia, as well as all the musician's other early losses, in his music. The titles, most notably "Julia," and the lyrics of many of his songs directly refer to his yearning and search for his mother. Lennon's music served as an external meeting ground with his lost mother just as Sarah's hammock and Phyllis's rock kept them linked to their losses.

You may recall that the linking objects of perennial mourners were described as a symptom of their inability to resolve grief. An art form that serves as a linking object has the same underlying psychodynamics. However, in the artist's case the creativity has lifted the dynamic (the search for and dread of reunion with the dead) to a higher level of human expression, to the arena of beauty and truth. Furthermore, Phyllis's rock had no meaning to anyone but Phyllis—an art form has the power to inspire others.

The attempt to compensate for a loss through a creative act is not limited to loss through death. As psychoanalyst William Niederland points out, the loss or threatened loss of a body part often spurs individuals to hone other talents, develop compensatory skills, or repair a hurt. The French painters Degas and Monet had limited eyesight. Sir Walter Scott, who was crippled by polio at age two, created literature's most invincible knight, Ivanhoe. Yeats wrote some of his most glorious poetry expressing dismay at his old age—and the loss of his youth. Niederland points out that the crippled painter Toulouse-Lautrec intuited painting's compensatory function in his life, "If my legs had been a little longer, I would never have become a painter."[4]

Let us return to Judy Jashinsky, whose *Sleeping Beauty* represents a triumph over her delayed mourning for her father. Jashinsky, who for many years could not paint a fully realized figure, painted a dead sailor to resolve her grief and then proceeded to paint a massive canvas of explorer Christopher Columbus, the world's most famous sailor-explorer, and his lively crew. I expect that Jashinsky will go on to explore new horizons in her art.

THE ENDING TO AN IMMIGRANT'S MOURNING

In 1969, I received a call from a policy group from the Brookings Institution studying the continuing tensions between Turks and Greeks on my home island, Cyprus. The policymakers were bewildered that these two cultures could not live in peace as a blended nation of Cypriots and asked me to present a speech about my boyhood on the island. As I tried to convey to them the fierce sense of identity and loyalty both groups had to their individual cultures, I heard myself reciting a litany of unresolved losses.

This experience at Brookings quickly involved me in the

burgeoning field of political psychology. In my work, I had many opportunities to meet with individuals on both sides of various ethnic or national conflicts. As I listened to heartbreaking stories of Northern Irish Catholics and Protestants, Tamils and Sinhalese of Sri Lanka, and Israelis and Palestinians, Azerbaijanis and Armenians, I kept hearing the language of loss and mourning and tales of hurts passing from generation to generation.[5] I increasingly found myself casting these political histories in terms of losses and gains, and so I began to seek out scholars to study how ethnic and national groups mourn. Yet my work did not really begin in earnest for nearly a decade. Although I did not know it at the time, there was a lingering issue that I needed to address, a loss still left to mourn—my identity as a Turkish-American and my adaptation to life in the United States.

It took me four years to "find" the vehicle for that mourning. It turned out to be a psychobiography of Atatürk, the father of modern Turkey, that I undertook in 1973 with my good friend, Norman Itzkowitz, a Princeton historian.[6] To a Turkish boy, Atatürk is the ultimate charismatic father figure, roughly comparable in the public imagination to a potent combination of George Washington, Abraham Lincoln, and John F. Kennedy. Even though I was aware that the topic would reverberate through me on several levels—my immigration to the United States and leaving behind my Cypriot Turkish culture, the recent death of my father, and the political unrest that daily jeopardized the lives of my friends and family—we envisioned that the project would take about eighteen months. Five years later, we finished. It was no accident that the writing took us so long. The odyssey of understanding Atatürk had led me to remourn my series of losses and to work out my issues around immigration. The night of the publication party, I dreamed that I was surrounded by newspapers in many foreign languages. However, the headlines were understandable to me because they were all the same: "Atatürk is dead," and I was sobbing. Atatürk represented my father, my Turkish identity, my traditions and roots. With the completion of that book and that dream, I had laid to rest old issues that lingered even after my analysis. I felt more comfortable and integrated as a Turkish-American.

Since that time, I have increasingly concentrated on political psychology. My focus is on how nations and ethnic groups mourn and what happens when a group cannot mourn, when a devastating war or other drastic loss leaves it unable to recover. The result is that the unresolved losses and the inability to mourn become part of the social and political process. I am optimistic that this sort of research will broaden the understanding of international relationships and play a role in facilitating peaceful management of political conflict. I know that my interest in this work partly stems from growing up in the conflict-torn island of Cyprus and represents an attempt to repair its wounds, just as surely as my earlier investigation into complicated mourning solved for me the riddle of my uncle's death.

Notes

INTRODUCTION

For details on Alice see Volkan, Vamık D. (1981).
Volkan, Vamık D. (1966, 1970, 1972, 1974, 1981, 1985); Volkan, Vamık D., Cillufo, Anthony, and Sarvay, Thomas (1975); Volkan, Vamık D., and Showalter, Robert 1968); Volkan, Vamık D., and Josephthal, Daniel (1980).

CHAPTER I

. Every researcher sees the same clinical phenomena. The classifications differ depending on the researcher's theoretical orientation. For example, John Bowlby (1961), a proponent of attachment theory, identified three phases of the mourning process although he and Colin Parkes (1970) later worked out a scheme with four. Bowlby and Parkes describe a first phase of numbness. This phase lasts from a few hours to a week. Numbness is followed by a phase of yearning for the lost person and the mourner's urge to recover the loss, which may last for a few months or years. The third phase is disorganization, followed by a fourth phase of reorganization.

George Pollock (1961) differentiates between acute and chronic stages of mourning. He then subdivides the acute stage into three subphases: shock reaction, affective reactions, and separation reaction. Pollock's chronic stage is similar to the classic work of mourning phase described by Sigmund Freud (1917). Volkan (1981) follows Pollock's model but does not use the terms acute and chronic. To avoid semantic difficulties, he divides the total mourning process into an initial stage and the work of mourning. He also emphasizes the adaptation process following grief as do Pollock (1961) and Gregory Rochlin (1965).

2. There are times, such as in an absence of grief reaction, that the individual does not feel distressed, as is discussed in Chapter 5.
3. Lindemann, Erich (1944).
4. *Newsweek*, January 2, (1989). "The Cruelest Kind of Grief," p. 21.
5. Erich Lindemann (1944) coined the term "anticipatory grief" to describe the way an individual moves through grief before the actual loss occurs. This is quite commonly seen in the families of terminal cancer patients and in the children of elderly parents.
6. Lewis, C. S. (1963), p. 1.
7. *Wall Street Journal*. July 7, (1989), p. 1.
8. Brandon, Heather (1984), pp. 318–319.
9. Ethnographic studies of grief show that from society to society there is notable consistency in reactions to loss. Rosenblatt (1975) applied content analytic research methods to ethnographic descriptions of seventy-eight societies from the Copper Eskimo to Chinese peasants and from the Basques of Spain to the Jivaro of the Amazon jungle. While emotional expressions differ from one group to another, people everywhere have grief reactions.
10. McGuire, Edna (1968), p. 91. See also Parkes, Colin M., and Weiss, Robert S. (1983), p. 244.
11. Caine, Lynn (1974), p. 99.
12. Videotape, "The Hidden Grievers," courtesy of St. Vincent's Hospital, New York, NY.
13. Miller, Arthur (1987), p. 531.
14. Lewis, C. S. (1963), p. 67.
15. Modern sleep studies show that normal sleep consists of two phases. The first is referred to as non-rapid eye movement (NREM.) After about ninety minutes of NREM sleep, the typical adult enters into a second phase of rapid eye movement (REM) sleep during which the central nervous system is enormously active, at times equaling or exceeding usual levels of activity of the waking state. In laboratory experiments, subjects awakened from REM sleep recall vivid dreams, as contrasted with rare reports of dreaming during the NREM period. REM phase occurs cyclically about every ninety minutes from four to six times during a typical night's sleep. Therefore, we now know we dream every night; however, we may not remember it after awakening.

    Some investigators have suggested that dream interpretation should be obsolete since dreaming is an obligatory neurophysiological function. And certainly some of Sigmund Freud's (1900) views of dreams need to be revised in light of modern dream research. But to consider dreams meaningless would be throwing the baby out with the bathwater. In order to understand the deeper meaning of any dream, it has to be analyzed in a proper therapeutic setting. However, the dreams' storylines (manifest contents) included here are intended to illustrate how a dream reflects an individual's involvement in mourning.

16. *New York Magazine*, Sept. 25 (1989), p. 94.
17. This dream was related to Dr. Volkan by Washington, D.C., psychoanalyst Dr. Rex Buxton.

CHAPTER II

1. Freud, Sigmund (1917).
2. Tähkä, Veikko (1984).
3. Freud, Sigmund (1917).
4. We coin the term psychic double for the purpose of this book. In psychoanalysis, the concept is known as *mental representation*.
5. Lewis, C. S. (1963), pp. 55–56.
6. Talbot, Toby (1980), p. 154.
7. Philipe, Anne (1963), p. 7.
8. Shakespeare, William, *King John*, Act III, Scene 4.
9. See for example: Osterweis, M., Solomon, F., and Green, M. (1984); Zisook, S. (1987); Glick, Ira O., Weiss, R. S., and Parkes, Colin M. (1974).
10. Obviously, losses vary in range and intensity and so do mournings. In divorce, the work of mourning takes a slightly different course than it does after a death because the former spouse is still available for interaction and the negotiating of a legal settlement becomes part and parcel of grief work. The chief difference between death and divorce is the ability to return for a real-world look at the former spouse; this limits fantasy and idealization and keeps the realistic reasons for the split center stage. The same dynamics apply in the grief of émigrés. A voluntary move from a homeland parallels grieving a divorce; one can return to the native land for a second look. Such return visits keep fantasy and idealization in check. A forced exile feels more like a death.
11. Caine, Lynn (1974), p. 95.
12. See Caine, Lynn (1974), p. 98.

13. Brandon, Heather (1984), p. 233.
14. Freud, Anna (1967).
15. Pollock, George H. (1961), p. 352.
16. William Faulkner quoted in Edel, Leon (1982).
17. Anniversary reactions relating to mourning are a fascinating subject. For an analysis of psychological meanings, see Pollock, George H. (1989).
18. Talbot, Toby (1980), pp. 178–179.

CHAPTER III

1. Kushner, Harold (1981), p. 133.
2. du Maurier, Daphne (1981), pp. 123–124.
3. Freud, Sigmund (1905). Identification begins in an attempt to fend off separation. A child becomes like his or her parents in an unconscious attempt to keep them close. The power of identifications was demonstrated by researchers who observed a group of one- and two-year-olds and their mothers in a laboratory/play space: When the mothers left the room, one quarter of the children climbed up into the chairs the mothers had vacated. Lewis, M., Feiring, C., and Weinraub, M. (1981).
4. Talbot, Toby (1980), p. 178.

CHAPTER IV

1. Volkan, Vamık D. (1979). I wrote about this period in a book on Cyprus.
2. Survivor guilt first came to attention after World War II when survivors of Nazi concentration camps provided psychoanalysts with an opportunity to study the inner worlds of those who survive natural or man-made disasters, including their conscious and unconscious guilt and their difficulty mourning and loosening attachments because of the guilt. See Niederland, William G. (1961, 1968).
3. Ironically, even a death following a prolonged illness can be experienced as sudden if it occurs at a time the survivor was not expecting it, for instance while he or she is on a brief vacation. Volkan, Vamık D. (1970).
4. Glick, Ira O., Weiss, R. S., and Parkes, Colin M. (1974).

5. Shanfield, Stephen B., Swain, B. J., and Benjamin, G. A. H. (1986–1987).
6. Feingold, Michael (1990), p. xii.
7. All quotations from men in the St. Vincent's support group are taken from the videotape "The Hidden Grievers," courtesy of St. Vincent's Hospital, New York, NY.
8. Monette, Paul (1988), p. 2.
9. "Struggling to Cope with the Losses as AIDS Rips Relationships Apart," *The New York Times*, Dec. 6, 1992, pp. A1, A32.
10. Ibid.
11. Wolfenstein, Martha (1966, 1969).
12. Blos, Peter (1968) described certain conditions which occur in adolescence. One of these is known as *the second individuation*, and it describes how the adolescent loosens his emotional ties to his infantile psychic doubles (representations) of his parents and important others. During the second individuation the adolescent appears to be in turmoil. See also Freud, Anna (1958).

CHAPTER V

1. It is fascinating to look at the way Jewish practices address the psychological needs of those survivors. Jewish rites do not call for ritual viewing of the body; however, at the graveside, mourners help shovel earth onto the casket, which forces acknowledgment of the death. Other traditional Jewish bereavement customs are understood as outward expressions of ways in which the loss has diminished the mourner's world.

   Mourning customs throughout the Western world dictate the bereaved family wear dark clothes for a two-year period, which corresponds to the approximate time it takes to adapt to the death. The clothes became progressively lighter as a signal that the mourner's grief was resolving and that he or she would soon be able to resume his or her place as a fully functioning member of society.
2. Mahler, Margaret S. (1968).
3. Deutsch, Helene (1937).
4. Bowlby, John (1980), pp. 153–156.
5. Tyler, Anne (1985), p. 142.

CHAPTER VI

1. Description of Queen Victoria from Strachey, Lytton (1921), pp. 296, 306; and Weintraub, Stanley (1987), p. 319.
2. Miller, Arthur (1987), pp. 34–35.
3. Duffy, Bruce (1990), pp. 70–71.
4. Baker, Russell (1989), p. 7.
5. There is a relationship between establishing an introject and creating a linking object. The introject is experienced within the body and, thus, the psychic double and the self interact. Once a colleague told me of a patient whose introject had moved onto her right shoulder—outside of her body but still attached. The linking object is the meeting ground of the externalized introject and the corresponding self-representation.
6. See Winnicott, D. W. (1953); Greenacre, Phyllis (1950); and Volkan, Vamık D. (1976).

CHAPTER VII

1. Parkes, Colin M. (1972).
2. Unhealthy identifications are also at work in the process known as Stockholm Syndrome, which occurs when victims begin to resemble their oppressors. A victim who has endured a trauma that damages or shuts down his psychic organization can lose the ability to draw on the early identifications that defined his personality. Broken and regressed, he seeks an authority figure with whom to identify and adopts the views of the guards or captors.
3. Steve's symptoms would be diagnosed as depressive equivalent, meaning that he exhibited the psychodynamics of clinical depression but did not present as depressed.
4. The analysis of this interesting man is the basis of my book *What Do You Get When You Cross a Dandelion with a Rose?* (1984).
5. It is sufficient for my purposes to repeat a statement by David R. Hawkins (1985), a psychoanalyst who has conducted significant research on the relationship between depression and sleep. According to Hawkins, depression cannot be traced to one or two single origins, rather it is the final common pathway for a number of basic abnormalities. Hawkins likens depression to diabetes mellitus, which is turning out to be a number of different disorders, all of which lead to ineffective functioning of the carbohydrate metabolism system and all of which

affect insulin function. Hawkins notes that psychosocial issues also play a role in the appearance of depression. I would add that the individual's intrapsychic organization (mind) plays a role as well and that this intrapsychic influence usually relates to an experience with a loss. It's obvious that many other psychosocial and intrapsychic events besides death cause depression. If biochemical and physiological factors dominate, the depression is said to be caused by nonpsychological influences. However, when these patients are analyzed, psychoanalysts always find psychological factors intertwined with the physiological ones.

6. Shakespeare, William, *Hamlet*.
7. Styron, William (1990).
8. Styron, William (1990).
9. Styron, William (1979).

CHAPTER VIII

1. This term was coined by Klein, Melanie (1946).
2. Shapiro, Edward R. et al. (1975).
3. Sigmund Freud's (1929) letter to Dr. Ludwig Binswanger. See Freud, Ernst L. (1960), p. 386.
4. Freud, Sigmund (1929).
5. Ascher, Barbara, *New York Times*, Nov. 19, (1989), p. 30.
6. For a detailed discussion of this topic, see Bowlby, John (1980); Raphael, Beverly (1982). See also Nagy, M. (1948); Piaget, Jean (1951); Furman, Robert (1973); Furman, Edna A. (1974).
7. Duffy, Bruce (1990), p. 71.
8. Dietrich, David R. (1989), p. 287.
9. Robinson, Marilynne (1980), p. 214.
10. Freud, Anna, and Burlingham, Dorothy (1942).
11. Freud, Anna (1967).
12. Reported by M. Rosenbaum in Nicholi, Armand M., Jr. (1988), p. 748.
13. This view is taken from Wakerman, Elyce (1987), p. 268. She cites Jordan, Ruth (1976), p. 56; and Williams, Juanita H. (1977), p. 45.

Notes

CHAPTER IX

1. Volkan, Vamık D. (1971, 1981, 1985); Volkan, Vamık D., and Showalter, Robert (1965).

CHAPTER X

1. A comprehensive examination of this subject can be found in Pollock, George (1989). Also see Niederland, William (1965, 1989).
2. Plath, Sylvia (1960), p. 224.
3. Julius, Demetrios, A. (1986).
4. Niederland, William G. (1989).
5. Rogers, Rita R. (1979). See also Volkan, Vamık D. (1988).
6. Volkan, Vamık D., and Itzkowitz, Norman (1984).

Bibliography

Baker, Russell. (1989). *The Good Times.* New York: William Morrow.

Birtchnell, J. (1972). Early parent death and psychiatric diagnosis. *Social Psychiatry* 7:202–210.

Blos, Peter. (1968). Character formation in adolescence. In *The Adolescence Passage,* pp. 171–191. New York: International Universities Press, 1979.

Bowlby, John. (1961). Process of mourning. *International Journal of Psycho-Analysis* 42:317–340.

Bowlby, John. (1980). *Attachment and Loss, Vol. 3: Loss: Sadness and Depression.* New York: Basic Books.

Brandon, Heather. (1984). *Casualties: Death in Vietnam; Anguish and Survival in America.* New York: St. Martin's Press.

Caine, Lynn. (1974). *Widow.* New York: William Morrow & Company, Inc.

Deutsch, Helene. (1937). Absence of grief. *Psychoanalytic Quarterly* 6:12–23.

Dickinson, Emily. (1935). *The Poems of Emily Dickinson.* Boston: Little, Brown & Co.

Dietrich, David R. (1989). Early childhood parent death, psychic trauma and organization, and object death. In *The Problem of Loss and Mourning: Psychoanalytic Perspectives,* ed. D. R. Dietrich and P. C. Shabad, pp. 277–335. Madison, Ct.: International Universities Press.

Duffy, Bruce. (1990). When a father dies. *Harper's Magazine,* June, pp. 70–71.

du Maurier, Daphne. (1981). *The Rebecca Notebook and Other Memories.* London: Victor Gollancz.

Edel, Leon. (1982). *Stuff of Sleep and Dreams.* New York: Harper & Row.

Bibliography

Eliot, T. S. (1971). *The Complete Poems and Plays.* New York: Harcourt Brace & World.

Feingold, Michael. (1990) Introduction. In *The Way We Live Now: American Plays and the AIDS Crisis*, ed. M. Elizabeth Osborn. New York: Theatre Communications.

Freud, Anna. (1958). Adolescence. *The Psychoanalytic Study of the Child* 13:255–278.

Freud, Anna. (1967). About losing and being lost. *The Psychoanalytic Study of the Child* 22:9–19.

Freud, Anna, and Burlingham, Dorothy. (1942). *War and Children.* New York: International Universities Press.

Freud, Ernst L., ed. (1960). *Letters of Sigmund Freud*, tr. Tania Stern and James Stern. New York: Basic Books.

Freud, Sigmund. (1900). The interpretation of dreams. *Standard Edition*, vols. 4 and 5.

Freud, Sigmund. (1905). Three essays on the theory of sexuality. *Standard Edition*, 7:130–243.

Freud, Sigmund. (1917). Mourning and melancholia. *Standard Edition*, 14:237–258.

Furman, Edna A. (1974). *A Child's Parent Dies: Studies in Childhood Bereavement.* New Haven, Ct.: Yale University Press.

Furman, Robert. (1973). A child's capacity for mourning. In *The Child in His Family: The Impact of Disease and Death*, Vol. 2, ed. E. J. Anthony and C. Koupernik, pp. 225–231. New York: John Wiley.

Glick, Ira O., Weiss, R. S. and Parkes, Colin M. (1974). *The First Year of Bereavement.* New York: John Wiley: Interscience.

Greenacre, Phyllis. (1970). The transitional object and the fetish: with special reference to the role of illusion. *International Journal of Psychoanalysis* 51:447–456.

Hawkins, David R. (1985). Sleep and depression. In *Depressive States and Their Treatment*, ed. V. Volkan, pp. 359–379. Northvale, N.J.: Jason Aronson.

Jordan, Ruth. (1976). *George Sand.* London: Constable.

Julius, Demetrios A. (1986). Mourning and melancholia in the creativity of John Lennon. Paper presented at the Virginia Psychoanalytic Society Annual Meeting, Charlottesville, Virginia, October.

Klein, Melanie. (1940). Mourning and its relation to manic-depressive states. *International Journal of Psycho-Analysis* 21:125–153.

Klein, Melanie. (1946). Notes on some schizoid mechanisms. *International Journal of Psycho-Analysis* 27:99–110.

Bibliography

Kushner, Harold S. (1981). *When Bad Things Happen to Good People.* New York: Schocken Books.

Leitner, Isabella. (1985). *Saving the Fragments.* New York: New American Library.

Lewis, C. S. (1963). *A Grief Observed.* London: Faber and Faber. New York: Bantam Books, 1976.

Lewis, M., Feiring, C., and Weinraub, M. (1981). The father as a member of the child's social network. In *The Role of the Father in Child Development*, ed. M. E. Lamb, pp. 259–264. New York: Wiley.

Lifton, Robert Jay. (1975). Preface. In *The Inability to Mourn,* A. Mitscherlich and M. Mitscherlich, pp. vii–xiii. New York: Grove.

Lindbergh, Anne Morrow. (1973). *Hour of Gold, Hour of Lead.* New York: Harcourt, Brace & Jovanovich.

Lindemann, Erich. (1944). Symptomatology and management of acute grief. *American Journal of Psychiatry* 101:141–148.

Mahler, Margaret S. (1968). *On Human Symbiosis and the Vicissitudes of Individuation.* New York: International Universities Press.

McGuire, Edna. (1968). *The Maoris of New Zealand.* New York: Macmillan.

Miller, Arthur. (1987). *Timebends: A Life.* New York: Grove Press.

Monette, Paul. (1988). *Borrowed Time: An AIDS Memoir.* New York: Harcourt, Brace & Jovanovich.

Nagera, H. (1970). Children's reactions to the death of important objects: A developmental approach. *Psychoanalytic Study of the Child* 25:360–400.

Nagy, M. (1948). The child's theories concerning death. *Journal of Genetic Psychology* 73:3–12.

Nicholi, Armand M., Jr. (1988). *The New Harvard Guide to Psychiatry.* Cambridge, Mass. and London: The Belknap Press of Harvard University.

Niederland, William G. (1961). The problem of the survivor. *The Journal of Hillside Hospital* 10:233–247.

Niederland, William G. (1965). An analytic inquiry into the life and work of Heinrich Schliemann. In *Drives, Affects, Behavior,* Vol. 2, ed. M. Schur, pp. 369–396. New York: International Universities Press.

Niederland, William G. (1968). Clinical observations on the survivor syndrome. *The International Journal of Psychoanalysis* 49:313–315.

Niederland, William G. (1989). Trauma, loss, restoration and creativity. In *The Problem of Loss and Mourning: Psychoanalytic Perspectives,* ed. D. R. Dietrich and P. C. Shabad, pp. 61–82. Madison, Ct.: International Universities Press.

Osterweiss, M., Solomon, F., and Green, M., eds. (1984). *Bereavement: Reactions, Consequences, and Care.* Washington, D.C.: National Academy Press.

Parkes, Colin M. (1972). *Bereavement: Studies of Grief in Adult Life.* New York: International Universities Press.

Parkes, Colin M., and Weiss, Robert S. (1983). *Recovery from Bereavement.* New York: Basic Books.

Philipe, Anne. (1963). *No Longer than a Sigh.* Paris: Rene Juilliard.

Piaget, Jean. (1951). *The Child's Conception of the World.* London: Routledge and Kegan Paul.

Plath, Sylvia. (1960). *The Collected Poems*, ed. Ted Hughes. New York: Harper & Row, 1981.

Pollock, George H. (1961). Mourning and Adaptation. *International Journal of Psycho-Analysis* 42:341–361.

Pollock, George H. (1989). *The Mourning-Liberation Process*, vols. 1 & 2. Madison, Ct.: International Universities Press.

Raphael, Beverly. (1982). *The Anatomy of Bereavement.* New York: Basic Books.

Robinson, Marilynne. (1980). *Housekeeping.* New York: Farrar Straus Giroux.

Rochlin, Gregory. (1965). *Griefs and Discontents: The Forces of Change.* Boston: Little, Brown & Co.

Rogers, Rita R. (1979). Intergenerational exchange: Transference of attitudes down generations. In *Modern Perspectives in the Psychiatry of Infancy*, ed. J. Howells, pp. 339–349. New York: Brunner/Mazel.

Rosenblatt, P. C. (1975). Uses of ethnography in understanding grief and mourning. In *Bereavement: Its psychosocial Aspects*, ed. B. Schoenberg, I. Gerber, A. Wiener, A. H. Kutscher, D. Peretz, and A. C. Carr, pp. 41–49. New York: Columbia University Press.

Shakespeare, William. (1981). *The Complete Works*, ed. G. B. Rison. New York: Harcourt, Brace & World.

Shanfield, Stephen B., Swain, B. J., and Benjamin, G. A. H. (1986–87). Parents' responses to the death of adult children from accidents and cancer: A comparison. *Omega* 17:289–297.

Shapiro, E. R., Zinner, J., Shapiro, R. L., and Berkowitz, D. A. (1975). The influence of family experience on borderline personality development. *International Review of Psycho-Analysis* 2:399–441.

Strachey, Lytton. (1921). *Queen Victoria*. New York: Harcourt, Brace and Company.

Styron, William. (1979). *Sophie's Choice*. New York: Random House.

Styron, William. (1990). *Darkness Visible: A Memoir of Madness*. New York: Random House.

Tähkä, Veikko. (1984). Dealing with object loss. *Scandinavian Psychoanalytic Review* 7:13–33.

Talbot, Toby. (1980). *A Book About My Mother*. New York: Farrar, Strauss & Giroux.

Tyler, Anne. (1985). *The Accidental Tourist*. New York: Alfred A. Knopf.

Viorst, Judith. (1986). *Necessary Losses*. New York: Simon & Schuster.

Volkan, Vamık D. (1966). Normal and pathological grief reactions. *Virginia Medical Monthly* 93:651–656.

Volkan, Vamık D. (1970). Typical findings in pathological grief. *The Psychiatric Quarterly* 44:231–250.

Volkan, Vamık D. (1971). A study of a patient's "re-grief work" through dreams, psychological tests and psychoanalysis. *Psychiatric Quarterly* 45:255–273.

Volkan, Vamık D. (1972). The "linking objects" of pathological mourners. *Archives of General Psychiatry* 27:215–222.

Volkan, Vamık D. (1974). Death, divorce and the physician. In *Marital and Sexual Counseling in Medical Practice*, eds. D. W. Abse, C. M. Nash, and L. M. R. Louden, pp. 446–462. New York: Harper & Row.

Volkan, Vamık D. (1976). *Primitive Internalized Object Relations: A Clinical Study of Schizophrenic, Borderline and Narcissistic Patients*. New York: International Universities Press.

Volkan, Vamık D. (1979). *Cyprus: War and Adaptation: A Psychoanalytic History of Two Ethnic Groups in Conflict*. Charlottesville, Va.: University Press of Virginia.

Volkan, Vamık D. (1981). *Linking Objects and Linking Phenomena: A Study of the Forms, Symptoms, Metapsychology and Therapy of Complicated Mourning*. New York: International Universities Press.

Volkan, Vamık D. (1982). Identification and related psychic events: Their appearance in therapy and their curative value. In *Curative Factors in Dynamic Psychotherapy*, ed. S. Slipp, pp. 153–176. New York: McGraw-Hill.

Volkan, Vamık D. (1984). *What Do You Get When You Cross a Dandelion with a Rose?: The True Story of a Psychoanalysis*. New York: Jason Aronson.

Bibliography

Volkan, Vamık D., ed. (1985). Psychotherapy of complicated mourning. In *Depressive States and Their Treatment*, pp. 271–295. Northvale, N.J.: Jason Aronson.

Volkan, Vamık D. (1988). *The Need to Have Enemies and Allies: From Clinical Practice to International Relationships*. Northvale, N. J.: Jason Aronson.

Volkan, V. D., Cilluffo, A. F., and Sarvay, T. L. (1975). Re-grief therapy and the function of the linking object as a key to stimulate emotionality. In *Emotional Flooding*, ed. P. Olsen, pp. 179–224. New York: Behavioral Publications.

Volkan, Vamık D. and Itzkowitz, N. (1984). *The Immortal Atatürk*. Chicago: University of Chicago Press.

Volkan, Vamık D. and Josephthal, D. (1980). The treatment of established pathological mourners. In *Specialized Techniques in Individual Psychotherapy*, ed. T. B. Karasu and L. Bellak, pp. 118–142. New York: Brunner/Mazel.

Volkan, Vamık D. and Showalter, R. C. (1968). Known object loss, disturbance in reality testing and "re-grief work" as a method of psychotherapy. *Psychiatric Quarterly* 42:358–374.

Wakerman, Elyce. (1987). *Father Loss: Daughters Discuss the Man That Got Away*. New York: Henry Holt and Co.

Weintraub, Stanley. (1987). *Queen Victoria: An Intimate Biography*. New York: E. P. Dutton.

Williams, Juanita H. (1977). *Psychology of Women: Behavior in a Bisocial Context*. New York: Norton.

Winnicott, Donald W. (1953). Transitional objects and transitional phenomena. *International Journal of Psycho-Analysis* 3: 89–97.

Wolfenstein, Martha. (1966). How mourning is possible. *Psychoanalytic Study of the Child* 21:93–123.

Wolfenstein, Martha. (1969). Loss, rage and repetition. *Psychoanalytic Study of the Child* 24:432–460.

Zisook, S. (1987). *Biological Aspects of Bereavement*. Washington, D.C.: American Psychiatric Press.

Index

Index

Index

Index

Index